T0317617

Trading between
the Lines

Since 1996, Bloomberg Press has published books for financial professionals on investing, economics, and policy affecting investors. Titles are written by leading practitioners and authorities, and have been translated into more than 20 languages.

The Bloomberg Financial Series provides both core reference knowledge and actionable information for financial professionals. The books are written by experts familiar with the work flows, challenges, and demands of investment professionals who trade the markets, manage money, and analyze investments in their capacity of growing and protecting wealth, hedging risk, and generating revenue.

For a list of available titles, please visit our Web site at www.wiley.com/go/bloombergpress.

Trading between the Lines

Pattern Recognition and Visualization of Markets

ELAINE KNUTH

WILEY

John Wiley & Sons, Inc.

Published by John Wiley & Sons, Inc., Hoboken, New Jersey. Published simultaneously in Canada.

For general information on our other products and services or for technical support, please contact our Customer Care Department within the United States at (800) 762-2974, outside the United States at (317) 572-3993 or fax (317) 572-4002. Wiley also publishes its books in a variety of electronic formats. Some content that appears in print may not be available in electronic formats. For more information about Wiley products, visit our Web site at www.wiley.com.

Library of Congress Cataloging-in-Publication Data:

Knuth, Elaine.
 Trading between the lines : pattern recognition and visualization of markets / Elaine Knuth.
     p. cm.—(Bloomberg financial series)
 Includes bibliographical references and index.
  ISBN 978-1-57660-373-4 (cloth); 978-1-118-04315-8 (ebk); 978-1-118-04316-5 (ebk); 978-0-470-87911-5 (ebk)
 1. Stocks—Charts, diagrams, etc. 2. Stocks—Prices—Charts, diagrams, etc.
 3. Technical analysis (Investment analysis) I. Title.
  HG4638.K58 2011
  332.63'2042—dc22

                                                                    2010053522

Printed in the United States of America

10 9 8 7 6 5 4 3 2 1

To Alexander
To the memory of my Parents

Contents

Preface

This book is more than a mere "how-to" guide to trading strategies. It is about conceptualizing price behavior so we can more easily recognize price pattern structures with predictive character to build our own trading tactics. Rather than finding discussions of "patterns that work," the reader will learn to recognize a pattern and build speculative trading tactics.

Before covering specific patterns, Chapters 1 and 2 challenge us to think about how we perceive our surroundings and what drives price and perception of price. Only with this can we then begin to think about what pattern recognition means, and how we can use the tools of pattern recognition.

Each pattern concept and constellation of a series of patterns throughout the book is first explained (framed) in a metaphor that fits the idea of the pattern. When reading about the *lightning bolt pattern*, for example, we first think about what conditions create lightning in the real world, and then within the context of this metaphor the pattern is described. Or when reading about the *Icarus pattern*, we first learn about what lead up to the mythological flight of Icarus. Beyond being simply a pattern name and description, the use of metaphor helps us better understand the concept behind a pattern. It is my hope that the reader will then adopt this method in visualizing and identifying additional predicative patterns for his or her own trading.

Readers will notice something else unusual to books on trading. There are few indicators on the charts throughout the book. This is deliberate. To keep a focus, charts are intentionally kept as simple and concentrated on price only as possible. Indicators are limited to occasional use of exponential moving averages, momentum, and an example of Wells Wilder's Average True Range (modified from his 14-period to a 20-period range). Our foremost purpose is consideration of price and pattern for analysis over indicators that are derivatives of price.

A reader might also ask, "Why does Don Quixote from Cervantes's *The Ingenious Hidalgo Don Quixote de la Mancha* appear throughout a book on market visualizations and patterns?" This literary work is episodic with a succession of events, much like the markets we are examining. Don Quixote was a "sane madman" who roamed the Spanish countryside as a "knight errant." He was adorned from head to foot with ridiculous armor and weapons in search of new and random adventures, prepared to battle against giants and evil (mostly in his imagination). He did all this for the rewards of recognition, honor, and the embrace of the lady love of his thoughts, Aldonza Lorenzo, or the name he conferred to her, Dulcinea del Toboso (a figure we never encounter as she is become, the "Holy Grail" of his mind). I found it fitting that our "sane madman" along with his "wise fool," Sancho Panza, accompany us as we look closely at the patterns of market episodes.

Acknowledgments

There are many whom I would like to thank and it is simply not possible to name everyone. Those I can include here are Guido Riolo, who first suggested that I might incorporate some of the ideas we had been discussing into a book, and Stephen Isaacs of Bloomberg Press, who found the project worthy. I thank Emilie Herman of John Wiley & Sons, who encouraged me to write with any approach I felt would work, unconventional as it may be; and Jennifer MacDonald and Stacey Fischkelta, whose energy, patience, and encouragement kept me on track throughout the project. I also wish to thank so many colleagues, from all over the globe, who, over the years and many discussions on the nature of open markets, pricing, and patterns, gave impulse to some of the ideas this book—including most recently ideas shared and debated with Irfan Polimac. Additionally, I must thank AQX Securities AG for tolerating late nights and weekends in their offices to see this project through. I am grateful for the technical help I received from Michael Krieger, who advised me on making sure that the charts and figures used throughout the book are of the highest quality possible; and to Lyle Andrews, as the 3-D visualization examples were generated from his fascinating product, Metaview.

CHAPTER 1

Perception and Pattern
How Mindset Affects
Understanding and Action

"Fortune is directing our affairs even better than we could have wished: for you can see over there, good friend, Sancho Panza, a place where stand thirty or more monstrous giants with whom I intend to fight a battle and whose lives I intend to take; and with the booty we shall begin to prosper . . ."

"What giants?" said Sancho Panza.

"Those giants that you can see over there," replied his master, "with long arms: there are giants with arms almost six miles long."

"Look you here," Sancho retorted, "those over there aren't giants, they're windmills, and what look to you like arms are sails . . ."

"It is perfectly clear," replied Don Quixote, "that you are but a raw novice in this matter of adventures. They are giants; and if you are frightened, you can take yourself away and say your prayers while I engage them in fierce and arduous combat."

—The Ingenious Hidalgo Don Quixote de la Mancha by
Miguel de Cervantes Saavedra. [Translated
by John Rutherford, Penguin Books,
London (2003), pp. 63–64.]

The cliché is that a picture is worth a thousand words. A picture, visual pattern, or chart tells us more than can be expressed in "just" a thousand words. It allows instant comprehension and associations, and evokes memory and insight. Yet it is also said that pictures have little value and are not to be trusted for real science. Maybe that is because when we see a picture or watch a film, we do not necessarily see the elephant in the room. We are blind to what is right in front of us while our emotions, convictions, and preconceived notions influence our perception. A little-known, but stunning, example of this is Ötzi the Iceman. Even though the Iceman's well-preserved 5,000-year-old remains were extensively x-rayed and examined by trained physicians immediately after they were found, it was almost a decade before scientists and specialists in diagnostics recognized the (obvious) arrow flint in his upper chest and shoulder. "How could we not have seen it!" the researchers asked.

Perhaps other theories were simply too seductive, leading them astray while the bland truth was right there in front of them. Whatever the reason, their oversight allowed years of uninformed speculation around the cause of the Iceman's death and demonstrates how blind we can be in the face of the hard visual truth right in front of us.

Perception Drives Response to Pattern

Oversights and missing what is right in front of us is why consideration of patterns in price is incomplete without thinking about how we perceive and our individual sensibility to visual information. How, then, does one's perception determine a recognizable pattern? And how will it trigger our actions in response to the pattern?

Let's think about something familiar. You are out hiking in the mountains on a warm fall day with a friend who is visiting from the Caribbean. He has never been in the Alps and you want to show him the glaciers, the cold streams, and the vast views. Suddenly the wind picks up, the air turns cold as it snaps against your face, and the sky turns dark. You've experienced this set of conditions and sensations in this setting before. You know the pattern of weather events and how it can unfold. You perceive a rapid weather change with a storm on the way and sense possible danger. You have a twinge of fear in your stomach. Yet your visitor thinks it's just an approaching rain shower that will cool things off and quickly pass as it always does in the island climate he is used to.

The pattern you both see is exactly the same. While your visitor is concentrating on his expected outcome (a refreshing rain), you concentrate on yours (a storm or maybe even a blizzard). Each of your expectations is built on your own set of experiences—your individual mindsets. Two hikers in the same setting, observing the same reality and the same set of stimuli, but their perceptions, interpretations, and responses are diametrically opposed. The hikers bring two utterly different sets of experiences, memories, expectations, and resulting emotional reactions to the exact same information.

So while you instinctively scramble for shelter, your visitor scratches his head wondering, "What's the big deal?" You react to the weather patterns on instinct. Your actions are automatic and based on understanding the scenario and knowing its potential outcome.

From this simple example, we clearly see how perception and individual sensibility drive our actions and are essential to understanding pattern recognition in life and, as we shall see, in the markets.

What Is Pattern Recognition?

Patterns are abstract, almost never exact, and many times exist only in our mind. We'll leave it to philosophers and physicists to debate the truth and nature of patterns, as well as whether a pattern is "real" or not. For our purposes, though, we can at least agree on the premise that while your perception may differ from mine, all of us can identify and define patterns in a multitude of areas—from the weather to the price action of soybeans.

So what makes up a pattern and what do we really mean when we talk about *pattern recognition*? Most simply, a pattern emerges when we take a set of data or observations and attempt to define and classify it based on perceived similarity. Pattern recognition is a basic step in the scientific method where we reduce information and observations into orderly arrangements, or classifications, so we can deduce *intelligent* abstractions (in this case, the ability to project, conclude, and abstract additional information from a set of classifications and patterns). With classifications of defined patterns we impose order onto existing structures and behavior, and make predictions and conclusions on everything from the weather to disease progression through a population, to price development over a specific period of time. The use of pattern recognition ranges from music to medicine, to biology, psychology, and economics. We also use it in simple ways in our daily lives when we unconsciously conceptualize patterns to create order out of what appears to be chaos, as we do when, for example, looking for our friend in a sea of people on a busy city square.

It is with pattern recognition that we can immediately comprehend vast amounts of information, make conclusions and decisions, and take confident action in an instant. Patterns deliver information and help us perceive change. An outbreak of malaria in a population where malaria has never occurred before tells us there is an infestation of malaria-infected mosquitoes in the region. The patterns of cirrus clouds on a sunny day appear in advance of a cold front.

Discerning patterns is essential to the higher order of human brain function, reasoning, and behavior. Elaborate skills for pattern recognition are unique to human innovation and creativity. And capitalizing on this ability for pattern recognition (using the right side of our brain) is what assures superior performance in all of our endeavors. In trading, pattern recognition is instinctive and key to the technical analysis of price. Every day we seek predictable order in the markets, to create order out of the chaos of price behavior. Without this, we could not function or act in the markets.

Descriptions of patterns in actively traded markets are not new. They have been around since the descriptions of price patterns in the form of candlestick charting methods created by the rice traders of Osaka in the 18th century, as well as the extensive work on general price patterns of equities in the 1920s, and throughout the 1940s (a time of oscillating markets that may hold similarities to the era we now appear to be entering).

Many traders are familiar with defined individual chart patterns and their descriptions, such as *wedges, head and shoulders, rounding tops,* the "three-day reversal" or *saucer bottoms,* and so on. We may have even worked with the concepts of *Elliot Wave, Fibonacci price ratios,* or *Gann Theory*—all of which add quantitative dimensions to price pattern analyses. To this, over the past decades, we have also added massive computer resources and applied technology to assist us with techniques of pattern recognition and to pull repeating patterns out of seemingly random processes.

In this book, we will concentrate on the representation of price by observing the visual footprints created by market participants. We will focus on the trail of prices resulting from forces of supply, demand, and human sensibility. And while there are various fundamental background influences on price, we will not concern ourselves very much with numerical-based indicators (which are derivatives of price).

This is not to say that technical indicators or statistical modeling of frequencies of a price event or pattern have little value, or that quantified evidence-based analysis cannot tell us anything. To the contrary, there is much value in tools that help us give structure to market information. These tools not only provide discipline, but can help give order and validity to our perceptions. However, even though statistical analysis of the frequency of a price event may give us a strong indication, it is merely that—an *indication* of its validity—and will never be absolute. As we will discover, we are in the business of trading *change.* The results of frequencies of a price may be statistically significant during a period of past time, but change continues to happen as events occur and the world revolves. Remember, we are not in the business of trading statistics, but rather of understanding the nature of change in price as markets evolve.

While technical indicators such as price momentum indicators or relative price strength have value and are logical methods to quantify the internals of price action, our interest will be to concentrate on a constellation of patterns in the context of overall market action, including background sentiment behind the price trail. The charts in the following chapters will have few indicators because we will be focusing solely on patterns and their associated trading strategies.

Some readers may challenge this method and ask, "Has this been back-tested? Can you prove the legitimacy of patterns with statistical frequency?" My answer is that science can be observed, measured, and quantified, but price patterns reflect human behavior. Statistical relationships are valid until there is a change or disturbance in the system observed. More so, our subject is random, in a state of constant change, and never predictable. Markets react to a constantly changing world with constant inputs of information such as events, very few of which can be anticipated with certainty at all times. Contrary to how markets and their participants behave, though, back tested trading systems are often built on absolutes.

Pattern Recognition Is a Tool

As market participants and traders, we seek to capitalize on *change*, not *static systems*. This leads us to the next question: Does pattern recognition work? This is akin to asking whether technical analysis works, or whether a scalpel will cure cancer. Like any tool, it works in the hands of the one with understanding of the subject, the tools, and adroitness of observation, and action. Success ultimately comes as a function of the creativity and skill of the user.

The question of whether technical analysis and pattern recognition work may not be the right one. Additionally, exact timing is almost impossible; we may accept the premise that there is no trading system that can beat the market over time. (If you believe that entirely, you'll probably want to stop reading now.) What is generally predictable, however, are the essential and constant characteristics of human behavior: the distinctions of our humanity—fear, greed, anxiety with uncertainty, pain aversion—these are all part of our innate wiring, and are reflected in price behavior and patterns over time. This we know. Understanding ourselves and our reactions against the unfolding market patterns driven by millions of individuals can give us clarity to the perception of the pattern, our comprehension of it, and our ability to create a bit of order out of the chaos. In short, discerning all of these different variables gives you *an edge*.

The Complexity of a Transaction

A pattern in the markets is built by the tracks of price. It offers to us a map of where the players have been and what they were thinking. So, what does that last numerical tick on your screen (price) really mean? It is the amount of money (or materials in the case of barter) paid for the exchange of a particular object, or goods, or services. But what is behind this number representing a price, which in turn symbolizes materials or money? *Price* is the meeting of what we ask for and what we get. For the buyer, price is somewhere between what we know now and what we anticipate to have value in the future. For the seller, it is what he is willing to receive in order to part from ownership at that point in time. Behind the motivations and thinking of the buyer and seller are emotions, facts, influences, and perceptions, and all this brings the two parties to the price point where a transaction takes place.

We learn that price is a reflection of supply and demand. (We'll think a bit later about the caveats on what we *learn*.) If more people want to buy a widget than the existing or expected supply, there is "price pressure," and prices move up. If we have reason to believe that there will be a greater demand than supply, or that supply will be disrupted, we want to buy and hold until we think buyers are satisfied. And a satisfied market slows the increase in prices or becomes static, where buyers and sellers are in balance and there is no sustained pressure in either direction. Then we have a pattern of a flat, "range-bound" market.

The converse of a market with upside pressure is when we have more sellers than buyers, creating downward pressure and falling prices, until the rate of selling decreases or flattens out as sellers are satisfied. You may be thinking to yourself, "Well, of course! This is obvious. It is all about supply and demand and maybe different or better information for one side of the transaction versus the other." If that were all there was to it, though, trading and investing would be simple. It would be merely about who had the best information.

This is the paradox. Trading is not and never will be simple. (If it were merely a factor of information, then we would not have witnessed, for example, the most informed institutions going bust against their own books in the banking crisis of 2008–2009.) Trading will never be easy because the influences on price are in constant flux—just as the collective human activity and sentiment behind the prices are in constant change. These things can never be quantified with absolute certainty no matter how hard we try, no matter how elaborate our models and methods, how fast our execution, or how sophisticated the algorithms we feed our powerful computers.

There is more: At times, even our notion of reality becomes distorted. Individuals and entire groups act on "wrong" perceptions and make mistakes. Markets and price reflect this irrationality in what proves to be *mispricing*. And this creates an opportunity for the one who can "see" when others are blinded. So we know that sentiment (or human sensibility) plays into price and that is why we see efforts to measure this with a degree of certainty. We try to quantify a *sentiment range* with indicators such as the VIX index, a measurement of volatility (also considered the *fear index*), the put-to-call ratio, or the statistics of the Commitments of Traders (COT) Reports published by the Commodity Futures Trading Commission each week.[1] These and similar indicators are used to try and gauge investor sentiment with quantitative numerical tools. The utility of quantifying sentiment with this kind of data, however, is subject to debate.

Pricing by the Mob

The study of herding behavior of market participants and the resulting mis-pricing is a growing field of behavioral economics. Markus Brunnermeier of Princeton University, for example, hopes to pioneer a form of *neuro-financial* research regarding herding behavior around price bubbles. This, and similar work by Hersh Shefrin of Santa Clara University, who pioneered much of the work in pricing behavior, is important because at times, and as the trail of prices unfolds, perceptions and herding behavior of market participants are the *only* influence on price. Fully understanding this dynamic and the tipping points in sentiment that can happen in a flash as the herd gets spooked and changes direction could be one of the holy grails we seek for the trader. We may not know where work like this will lead us in the academic realm, but the experienced trader seeks to recognize this behavior and the telltale signs and patterns—not only patterns of price action but the behavior patterns of the participants, including the analysts and pundits (the human herd) driving price.

With pattern recognition tools we can identify the footprints of pan-icked crowds in the market. And as the hunter/trader, we can predict with a degree of reliability how this panic will play out as the herd is driven by universal human emotions. As long as irrational exuberance is a part of the human condition, bubbles will be with us. A symptom and pattern of this is, for example, the assumption that old limits have yielded to new and previously undreamed-of possibilities. We have all read how the Dow will always rise, as will housing prices, and that all energy will be based on ethanol and corn and prices will go up forever as the population and energy needs expand. (I still remember being told in 1988 that the Nikkei would never go down as it was structurally impossible due to the unique nature of the Japanese economy.) These and other market adages and cultural memes will never be absolute givens.

As traders and investors, we can exploit the human dynamics of price if we are tuned into the nature of why we repeat market memes (to give us emotional security in the face of unknowns. What triggers fear, exuber-ance, and greed in both ourselves and the crowd? Naturally and inevitably, we humans do get out of whack and when that happens, so will price. Recognizable patterns of price and behavior will emerge. It is then that the tracks of the market will scream out to us on the charts. When *that* happens we have an opportunity (sometimes a fabulous trading or investing opportunity) sitting right in front of us. But to act on it we have to be like Sancho Panza and see what is there no matter what a particular authority or the crowd tells us. We have to stand apart to get a view away from the thundering herd and see for ourselves; as we remove ourselves from the distractions and put our own plan into action.

It's Never Simple

This all sounds straightforward, even easy: identify a pattern, shut out the distractions, throw away the newsletters, turn off the talking heads, make your own interpretation, and take decisive action without all the thinking.

Computers already help us do this. Defining the metrics of a pattern and identifying it are straightforward. Trades then can be generated automatically. But think about it: Is the pattern our computer identifies a dog or a pony—a Kurdish Kangal or a Chincoteague pony? A double or triple top in the chart? From what point in time and how? The computer may not be able to rapidly distinguish this any more than it can differentiate among the very slight, but highly significant, differences in any time series or object. But you and I instantaneously perceive subtleties in the pattern of the objects identified so we can act. Humans share a unique and highly developed capability that no computer can match. Even today, it still takes tremendous supercomputer power to recognize the simplest of patterns.

Take computer recognition of a human face. That alone may be simple enough, but can the computer recognize whether it is the face of a boy or a girl? Is it a small child, adolescent, or adult? Is it human or simply a lifelike doll? When looking at the pattern, you and I can answer these questions and more—such as the approximate age, gender, and ethnicity of the face—in an instant. As humans, we have a vast constellation of patterns of information and memory that gives us a complete picture and a depth and wealth of information. And we can also make new associations among sets of information.

This is the massive analytical power we bring to observing and analyzing the markets. No computer can match it and only the human mind can reason in this intelligent way. Even more, the human can consider the significance of new information, missing information, or emerging patterns of information. We can project possible scenarios of outcomes as far as our rational imagination allows—and not only based on past occurrences, but by understanding the significance and implications of current events that may ultimately play into price. So why do we continue to put our faith and immense resources into computers for critical decision making about the markets?

We use computers to assist in coping with large abstractions and to order massive amounts of data. The tools of computers "crunch" data into order; they create models and projections based on geometry or statistical pattern recognition arrays. These tools then give us security in the absolutes we humans seek. And in some fields, these tools can do this with a good degree of precision.

Computers deal with the cold, hard facts we feed them. They do not get tired or suffer any cognitive dissonance. They do not impose subjective human judgment when we seek only impartial results.

The other side of the enormous and uniquely powerful human capability just described is human weaknesses. Computer generation rules compensate for our fears, anxieties, hopes, greed, desires, and misplaced expectations. For instance, when we find ourselves in trades and market conditions we do not understand or have never seen before, we might enter a state of indecision. We block out significant but uncomfortable information as we look around for confirmation of our expectations and hopes in order to justify staying with the trade. And yet we expose capital under these conditions. (Some of us may know traders who emotionally expose even more capital to this questionable trade to prove themselves "right" and the market "wrong.") With this often destructive behavior, we impose ourselves and our humanity onto perceptions of patterns. The computer does not.

Is Market-Delivered Data for Real Science?

There is something else. In the modern world, we are educated to believe that if we have enough data and facts, we can arrive at the truth, whereas in the ancient world, we dealt with (and accepted) large abstractions and unknowns; little was understood or even conceived as rational or literal and stories were told as metaphors to represent and conceptualize larger meanings. Since the "Age of the Enlightenment" of the late 17th century, we have taken the printed word for literal value and sought truth in the written word as fact and in numbers. Yet paradoxically even in physics and mathematics we deal with approximations. The ratio of the circumference of a circle to its diameter will never come to an even number. Its value can never be expressed exactly and even though it can be expressed to thousands of decimal places, we will never have the complete answer. We use computers even though quantum physics shows us that certain observations cannot be predicted absolutely. Instead, there is a range of possible observations each with a different probable outcome.

And so it is in the markets. We will never have all the data because total knowledge does not exist. We are constantly challenged with a flow of new information and change. (Remember: The *unknown* and *change* are what we are trading.) We must accept that if looking for greater absolutes or exactly what to do next for a positive outcome, we will have to go into another field.

In spite of this, there are more reasons we do trust the answer from a computer. For example, when we see a threat that may be too great to bear, we use psychological mechanisms to reduce it or block it out. This can be destructive, but is also a strong psychological survival mechanism. Traders might also do this when observing information and patterns that are dissonant to their expectations or beliefs, financial well-being, or job security. Blocking out threatening information is a side of humanity we discussed earlier. Some information, especially information we tend to block out, is simply too much to manage and still function within the chaos of ever-changing market conditions. A computer is objective and will gauge all information thrown at it. We create programs of rule-based interpretations and instructions in hopes of overriding the human failings of perception. The price we pay for this, though, is the loss of our immense human capacity for interpretive recognition of patterns. Is it possible to have both the efficient, tireless computer *and* the insight of humanity? Yes, perhaps to a degree we can train ourselves to overcome our human tendencies that hold us back and be sternly objective, while maintaining our natural abilities for extraordinary insight.

We can start by critically thinking about, for example, the tendency of even the most professional traders to build an entire strategy on a statistical probability of past occurrences. We must instead ask ourselves, What do we do when there is a gradual structural change to the market? What do we do when the outlier event occurs? What about an event that was not supposed to happen or one we could not have imagined? Do we have the tools to deal with this change? Do we blame the event, the change, or the inability of our system to adjust? Do we blame the indicators that did not capture the reality of the market. Even though we know, logically, that the markets' behavior is not science (where an experiment can be repeated over and over again in exactly the same setting and with the same materials and methods and where the results can be repeated to give real evidence of proof). No, markets are not laboratories where conditions are controlled, but arenas of human interaction undergoing constant change. And do we understand this change as risk or opportunity? Do we know what to do next?

Finally, as Warren Buffett said, "Risk comes from not knowing what you're doing," which is another way of saying not knowing what to do next. (For more about risk considerations against the patterns we trade, see Chapter 9.) We may not know exactly where the market will go next, but through ritualized methods of observation we can develop skills of recognition with systematic rules of observation, practice, and action as market scenarios unfold. We can develop a method of observation and strategic action. With this we can become a little bit more like the computer and train ourselves to know what to do next as market prices and patterns emerge.

What Distorts Perception

There is something else that can distort our perception or stand in the way of observation, understanding, and strategies. Not only can ignoring the information around us or creating false realities to make us happy be detrimental, but there is also a blindness that comes with having too much knowledge. For example, if we've been trained to believe that X always equals Y and that it is the absolute truth, and then suddenly we have information in front of us telling us that X actually equals Z, we will choose to ignore it. "Impossible," we say. X always equals Y: it is our only experience. Like our visitor on the Alpine hike at the beginning of the chapter, it is the only reality we know. However, a principle to consider both in markets and in life is, "We ignore information contrary to our own beliefs (and learned knowledge) at our own peril."

Two Monkeys

What makes the development of market price pattern-recognition skills even tougher is that we enter the marketplace with two great big monkeys sitting on our back: Hope and Greed. (We've heard about them so much it is cliché.)

With hope, there is a difference (and it can be difficult to distinguish) between healthy, independent thinking (standing outside of the group) and stubborn delusion, or even worse—the blind hope that can lead to denial and destructive actions. When this kind of hope is in control, we watch the unfolding reality of the market with our wishes and expectations imposed on it. Our desires (ego) control our perception of how the market is behaving. We cannot act on the real price information and patterns the market may give us because we do not see them. The monkey of hope is in the way, driving us to act solely based on what we hope, expect, and want from the market.

When does healthy motivation turn into motivation controlled by greed? Is your strategy built on trading for the big hit? Did you just sustain a larger loss than you ever imagined and find yourself trying to immediately get back into the market and "make it all back"? Does it become personal—between you and the market? If you step back and ask yourself these questions and find your answers along those lines, guess what? The monkey of greed is sitting on your back and he is the one pulling all the levers with each trade—not you.

When either or even both of these two monkeys are in control, it is only a matter of time before they cause your assured destruction. No player is too small or too sophisticated for the monkeys of blind hope and greed to find their way into your shop. Entire banking and governing structures or even an economy are not too large or sophisticated for greed to be in control.

For example, the well-documented and spectacular Long-Term Capital Management (LTCM) meltdown of 1998 remains a public case in point where these two monkeys were at play and in control. Simply put, what partially led to this crash was the exploitation of the fixed-income interest rate convergence among bonds issued at different dates observed over the previous few years. The strategy was built on *expectations* and *assumptions* that markets would behave *exactly* as they had in the past, and with little regard to the leverage required to reap the intended rewards as the size of the traded strategy grew. (Add to this the fact that there was no consideration given to the idea that markets do change.) Leverage increased to squeeze profits out of the ever-shrinking convergence spread until there were none to be had, and trading managers then entered trades outside of the basic strategy of bond arbitrage. New external influences came into the market and there was no strategy. No one knew what to do next under the pressure for performance and in the face of unknowns; and the fortunes of LTCM rapidly collapsed.

In this example, institutional investors followed each other and piled in, and when the market behaved outside of the perceived or expected pattern, information pointing to the flaws of the strategy was ignored and described as a temporary anomaly or simply not possible. (The monkey of hope was now working the levers.) Unfolding events proved that the risk of the entire portfolio was systemic and beyond imagination. In short, a *theoretical* model of the patterns of exact market behavior was used as a description of reality and acted upon as such. Ascribing the theoretical to the practical enabled participants to risk billions of dollars; information was ignored because it was not what we were taught or believed to be true. And in fact it was something new and contrary to our expectations and hopes. The dynamics at play here—ignoring new information, focusing on expectations (greed) and hopes, believing in delusions on a grand scale—are not merely limited to the behavior of a single trader or organization, but apply even to the broader economy, including the behavior of the most seemingly rational people, groups, and societies.

When we think back, wasn't it absolutely illogical in 2005 to believe that the ever-growing mountain of subprime loans and resulting derivative products could be sustained? Was it logical to believe that the trajectory of housing prices would only continue upward, no matter who told us that? Or that flipping ownership on homes (with 5% down made on a credit card) was the path to riches and would increase your wealth? Or that "building credit"—a euphemism for piling on personal debt—is good for everyone?

Was it economically rational that mortgage products were being packaged into *collateralized debt obligations (CDOs)*, with a bit of prime sprinkled into them, only to be sold off to European and Asian insurance companies? No, but because there was no history, no past *pattern* to understand the characteristics of subprime lending and the derivative CDO industry (one could not even get a quote on a screen for a CDO back in 2006), logical conclusions could not be made. Dissonant information was just a blip on the radar for the market participants. Why? It is a characteristic pattern of bubbles that logical questions or information counter to the expectations are ignored. Why was information rejected by highly sophisticated players? It was mostly because those on the backside of the CDOs were getting paid very well for their troubles; a perception (or rather, delusion) was created to justify being at the party. An imagined reality with a crowd of agreeing participants, each encouraging the others, was created.

Examples like these are the result of marketplace behavior where humans reject information right in front of their eyes because it is contrary to what they want to believe. Even the economists at the FDIC whose trained eyes identified the dark clouds over the mortgage market dismissed the meaning of this message when it was right in front of them—they ignored the significance of the data on the increase of undocumented loans, merely stating that "high-risk borrowers would not be able to meet mortgage payments."[2] Astoundingly, the risk to lending institutions and households (which are the crux of economic health) was not considered. "Lenders have targeted a wider spectrum of consumers (read: consumers of home mortgage loans), who may not fully understand the embedded risks but use the loans to close the affordability gap,"[3] the FDIC wrote. In the summer of 2006, the FDIC published a report stating the following:

> *Finally, if a recession or other severe economic shock were to send local home prices and incomes sharply lower, or interest rates sharply higher, this additional stress could contribute to higher mortgage losses.*
>
> *However, banks and thrifts will head into the next phase of the mortgage credit cycle from a position of strength. In recent years, the industry has generated record earnings and reached near-record capital levels. Given a gradual transition to higher delinquency and foreclosure rates and assuming only modest potential declines in collateral values, it does not appear at this time that deteriorating mortgage credit performance would present unmanageable risks to most FDIC-insured institutions.[4]*

Even though there was evidence to the contrary as well as logical conclusions of systemic risk, the information was blatantly dismissed. Like the flint arrow in the shoulder of Ötzi the Iceman (presented at the beginning of the chapter), the facts of Figure 1.1 presented in the very same report simply did not register. The chart reveals a hard-to-ignore, in-your-face visual meaning that the report's supporting text simply does not illuminate.

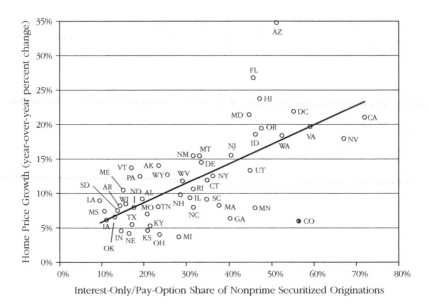

FIGURE 1.1 Nontraditional Mortgage Products Are Most Popular in States with the Strongest Home Price Growth
Source: Office of Federal Housing Enterprise Oversight; Loan Performance Corporation (Alt-A and B&C securities database).

It appears that all of the actual information in front of the authors of this report from the FDIC (and available to many others) was documented and then brushed away with the classical "wishful thinking." All of the participants—the best and the brightest—found a reason to believe that "this time it is different"; the markets are now much more sophisticated and so well-developed that risk is eliminated. To think and act otherwise would mean being outside of the crowd, rejecting conclusions made by an authority; and that was fraught with unknown risks. Safety, our human instincts tell us, is found within the group; this is the reason for often disastrous "groupthink."

Breaking Habits and Building Scenarios

How, then, do we break out of the cycle to clearly and openly observe, perceive, and take action, even when this demands that we act outside of or against our group? First, to see clearly, we can reduce representations of price change to the essential visual image of the abstraction of price and time. Through charts, we will identify correlations among pattern constellations and develop a framework of potential outcomes resulting from the identified patterns. Instead of probabilities, we'll think about steps we can take with *possible* (and seemingly impossible) scenarios. For example, before entering a transaction I think about trade scenarios instead of probabilities of outcome, since we are trading *perceived change* and not *probabilities*. This encourages a mental openness to the changing (and even dissonant) information the market delivers. For scenario building to work in our favor, we must first consider the scenarios we want to avoid. Preparing yourself for an undesirable outcome is not pessimistic or negative. It puts you in control of your actions as a particular (even worst-case) scenario unfolds, and puts you ahead of the game. With this approach, your risk is greatly reduced. You know what to do.

Building scenarios of price and changes in the markets (both *for* you and *against* you) helps you become a little less of a victim of human limitations and better able to recognize the information for what it could be *earlier* than most. Just like the cold commander in a chaotic, ever-changing battlefield, you have removed the expectations of probabilities and desires and instead opened your eyes and mind to the early warning patterns. (We will discuss the unfolding patterns—with scenarios both *for* and *against* your trade—in several of the next chapters.)

Establishing Rituals

Alongside scenario building, we can also rely on methods such as practice or "plays." I will refer to practice as *rituals* (or *trading rituals*) from here on; just as people have seasonally related rituals (as in religion, for instance) that help us navigate the seasons of the year, the phases of life, and the great unknowns, we can hone trading rituals to securely and instinctively navigate the markets.

Cultural rituals give us order and direction through the unknown. This is how we are wired. The sense of ritual became highly developed as nomadic peoples crossed the African planes on the way to the Arabian Peninsula and into the steppes of China (as the theory goes). Along that journey they were constantly dealing with change and dangerous unknowns. Rituals are created around patterns of seasons, birth, life, and death to give order, direction, and a degree of control through extremely harsh conditions. Rituals give us a method for moving forward through the unknown and to survive. They guide us in what to do next. Traders deal with constant unknowns and we need methods to give us order, direction, and control over the chaos.

Rituals also help us identify and build patterns with which we then conceptualize our world. This gives us perceived understanding and with this we can act upon and navigate our surroundings. It is how we create order out of chaos and build a framework to guide our actions. The more sound our framework (our conceptualization), the more effective our actions and successful our trading and investing will be over time. This personal edge is independent of access to information, computing power, execution speed, or quantitative testing of mathematically based indicators.

Before building your sound trading rituals, ask yourself the following questions. Do you seek reinforcement for your decisions? Do you need approval to support your decision making after your trade is taken, remaining within the safety of the crowd? Or do you find yourself seeking a reality check with the use of indicators? Do you continue until you find one and tweak it until it fits your hopes and expectations? And if that does not work, do you make a call to a trader friend (especially one who thinks just like you)? Or do you instead routinely and critically question yourself? (Why do you enter a trade, what is your plan, and are you still on track?) Has any of the information that caused you to take a trade changed? Do you have new information? Do you still have a plan at any given moment? Do you know and stick by your daily mental trading ritual? Do you ask yourself if you have blocked out any information that is contrary to your beliefs? Have you disregarded dissonant information? We need to critically question ourselves in these areas to make sure our perceptions are as balanced as possible when capital is at stake.

It is through such mental rituals and encouraging your innate abilities to navigate the markets instead of repressing them that will give you the advantage over much of the universe of market participants.

Conclusion

A price exists when two parties take action in agreement. Price action is triggered by human desires, needs, and wishes. Real price always reflects this, and a price series will create a pattern of emotions in the marketplace over time. As markets are arenas of ever-changing human folly, we can discern patterns of behavior in price and in turn build a strategy of action on our observations of participants and price. To overcome our own human limitations and develop a method of knowing what to do, we can ritualize how we approach and take action in the markets. And with this, we can stand aside from the crowd and clearly see the truth of the market through the ever-similar patterns of price action.

Finally, there are an infinite number of similar pattern possibilities and a few hundred that an effective trading strategy could be built upon. (Some might even say that there are thousands of patterns lending themselves to a theoretical trading strategy.) Yet, like the patterns of clouds predicting a weather front with perhaps hundreds of similar and identifiable patterns, no two are ever exactly alike. In the succeeding chapters, rather than limiting ourselves to single patterns in isolation, we will examine a series of patterns in a complete context, including their relationship to each other. Just as the experienced physician cannot make a complete diagnosis of a persistent headache without looking at the whole patient (including what may be weighing on his or her heart and mind), we cannot make a complete pattern diagnosis considering merely a brief period of time and price for a trade.

Rather than forecast, we will observe unstable price and pattern behavior to visualize possible future price direction as a market undergoes change. We will look inside ourselves, observe the crowd around us, and build price development scenarios, starting out with the least favorable. We will then take action based on the actual unfolding price events. The most important tools we have will be our eyes, for pattern recognition, and our mind, which can abstract and identify market delivered price information and constellations in an instant.

Visualizing the Concept of What Makes a Price

"For God's sake!" said Sancho. "Didn't I tell you to be careful what you were doing, didn't I tell you they were only windmills? And only someone with windmills on the brain could have failed to see that!"

"Not at all, Friend Sancho," replied Don Quixote. "Affairs of war, even more than others, are subject to continual change. All the more so as I believe, indeed, I am certain, that the same sage Freston who stole my library and my books and has just turned these giants into windmills to deprive me of the glory of my victory . . ."

—The Ingenious Hidalgo Don Quixote de la Mancha by Miguel de Cervantes Saavedra.
[Translated by John Rutherford, Penguin Books, London (2003), pp. 63–64.]

The market is not a meeting of bits of data moving in Brownian motion or passively and randomly in an empty abstract space as some elaborate explanations of price action may theorize. It is an *ordered system of exchange*, where participants are driven by individual responses to information.

The fuel or energy of the market is provided by information, which propels participants to take action. And the numerical symbol of price marks this action of exchange. Without this structure, the market would be as random and unstructured as the working of a computer without software, or walking in an unknown city without sight, hearing, sense of smell, or the ability to speak.

Price and the patterns emerging from a series of prices give us instruction; they are our guide.

In this chapter we think about the semantics of price: How do we perceive the markets? What influences perceived value (or the *named price*)? What are the triggers for action to create a price in the collective market? What are the metrics of value and price and what are some of the ways we can visualize them? And can price be predicted?

The Semantics of Price

When thinking about price, we assume it reflects a transaction in a transparent and informed market without the collusion of a group of bidders. And that price is informed and *not* random. We could say that at times, price data delivered to us may not be a reflection of all the collective knowledge. Instead, it is a reaction to the most dominant forces of information and human nature. Further, that price reflects the action and thinking of the strongest members of the "herd" in the marketplace, or what we will call the "dominant tribe."

Let's think about this. When asking for a price, most of us think the answer is a number. In recent decades, our ability to quantify a price series into greater abstractions has so greatly increased that we might think less and less about what the actual number represents. We might also visualize this number printed on paper or flashing across a computer screen. In trading, the number records a point of exchange. To bring the number associated with the exchange into perspective (to give it structure and relative meaning), we consider the point of exchange in relation to the exchanges preceding it (meaning, the *prices in the past*). With this visualization, a chain of hundreds, thousands, or even hundreds of thousands of past prices over time can be compiled into the context of an order where each of the prices (or *tick*) represents a point of transaction. It is in this context of hundreds of thousands of prices *relative to each other* in a chart or graph that we create a visual structure around a perceived order in the past to make trading decisions in the present and future.

All language, including the language of a price series, whether spoken or written, is representational. Like a single price, a single letter or word outside of its context tells us almost nothing. To understand the letter or word, we need to see it as part of a meaningful pattern, positioned within a series of letters abstracting a pattern of language. The pattern of letters together makes a word and its sound evokes the actual thing, thought, or idea it represents. But by itself the word tells only part of the story. We need more and logically connected words to fully understand a message. So we link the word with other words and create a chain in a recognizable pattern to make a sentence and complete a thought. And only by stringing many sentences together into a story within a complete context can we have greater insight and understanding into larger themes.

We can also think about price in the same way. Like a single letter, a single price outside of its context (of past prices and information around the price) has little or no meaning as there is no pattern or logical context.

When a string of prices are tracked and presented visually, it gives us much more information—a complete story of the market. We can then make associations as we do with written words or the sounds of speech. When we organize bits of information like a price series, this string takes on complex meaning and reveals recognizable and repeatable patterns.

Our Concept of Price Affects Our Understanding of Value

A price is a symbolic representation of a transaction, and the symbols we use to show price influence how we think or even behave in response to the transaction behind the price.

Theoretically, we could use any metric for price, but in reality we have measurements of price only to the degree practical for the purpose of the transaction. This changes over time and more often than we might realize. For example, in the 1950s, U.S. stocks were still priced to $\frac{1}{8}$ of one dollar (12.50 cents) and only later to $\frac{1}{16}$ of one dollar (6.25 cents) as opposed to the $\frac{1}{100}$ of one dollar (one cent) we now take for granted. For many, this might now seem unimaginable, but there are historical reasons for this.

In the early years of the American colonies, Spanish coins were in circulation. The coins were often cut into fractions: $\frac{1}{2}$, $\frac{1}{4}$, $\frac{1}{8}$. (The Romans also did this during inflationary periods and among their many far-flung outposts). Perhaps when thinking about coins still in circulation for exchange, and to establish a precise measurement of a trade, the New York Stock Exchange began trading shares in $\frac{1}{8}$ of one unit. It was the metric of the time because that is how the early traders under the Buttonwood tree thought about price: as actual bits of a physical coin. This system was based on something completely logical then, although it is a quaint and inefficient measurement of equity exchange for us now.

This concept of price around the physical metric of a coin determined pricing of equity transactions in North America until 2000. A one-eighth interval meant a 12.50-cent spread between a bid and ask. When this was clearly not precise enough as markets advanced, the exchanges went to $\frac{1}{16}$, doubling the price points of trade and allowing for a narrower spread. In the early 1950s, there were pushes to go to decimalization but it did not happen until well over half a century later, because a spread of 12.50 or 6.25

appeared—at least on the surface and in the short run—to serve the industry very well. Wall Street successfully resisted moves to decimalization, arguing it would encourage front running. The case made was that pros could step in front of the public simply by paying just a penny more. With such small spreads there would be price limit orders and the public would get squeezed out of the opportunity for transaction. These arguments were accepted for well over 50 years, maybe because industry regulators could not imagine a different pricing scheme. And at a time when many had individual equities in their portfolios and few funds, it was difficult for the average investor to conceptualize the significance of paying a spread of 6.25 or 12.5 cents per share! In time, however, the decimalization was finally adopted by way of the growing predominance of the fund industry—an industry run by professionals trained to understand and execute the most efficient transactions possible.

Now, with modern order entry applications where depth of an order book is shown to the individual trader, the arguments *against* decimalization (widely accepted just 20 years ago) seem absurd. What was completely logical hundreds of years ago—and even though it successfully outlived modern pricing logic and was accepted for so long it actually hindered exchange and competitiveness—was replaced by a more efficient price discreteness, a conceptualization of price that fits the tools of the modern industry and not the smelter of a mint.

In short, the price we imagine, see, and talk about is the symbolic measurement we happen to adopt at the time and for whatever reason. Of course it is possible to measure into ever greater and more discrete units. But a higher degree of accuracy is neither necessary nor efficient and would merely introduce an irrelevant unit of measurement—that is, until it does not. Three hundred years from now, decimalization may seem as quaint, inefficient, and unrepresentative of price as the fractions derived from the cut-off bits of a coin do to us now.

The abstractions and metrics we use to represent exchanges determine our understanding of price and in turn our conceptualization and visualization of an exchange or the patterns behind the price of the exchange.

Translating Price into Value

Does price, then, no matter how we understand and symbolize it (a stone, a bit of a coin, a binary impulse) translate to value? Does one even have anything to do with the other? I'd say yes if the value, or worth, is what "the market" determines something to be worth at a specific point in time (i.e., the price means the value).

For equities, we learn that the value of an enterprise is determined by its balance sheet—assets less liabilities divided by shares outstanding.

But there also could be more to it. What about the estimated worth of all assets minus depreciation and plus patents that factor into earnings times a multiple? Are the estimated earnings projected into the future used to establish a price now? Is value determined by records of past performance and earnings, or multiples of dividends? Taking various considerations into account, ask three analysts these questions about pricing equities and you will get three different answers about value and what the "right price" should be.

Outside of equity valuation, we are also taught in basic economics that value is measured by the degree of utility. The higher the cost to manufacture a widget and the higher the utility of the widget, the greater the value. This association is easy enough to understand and has appeal because it is something we can readily measure, even with simple arithmetic. Perhaps this is why it is widely adopted as a definition of value.

But wait: Wouldn't this make gold of little value, or (*gasp!*) even worthless? What about intellectual property? What is the price of an idea that we *think* will create value?

Gold has little if any utility on its own, and an idea is only that—an idea. It does not have *proven* utility. Yet society assigns a relative price to gold at any given time that it doesn't inherently possess. As for ideas, we will sometimes pay great sums for what we think is a great idea with future utility. We have thousands of patents on ideas for widgets and even methods and procedures that are still unproven thoughts on paper.

Quite clearly, utility alone does not mean value. There may never be an agreement on value or price. Economists, philosophers, and traders can carry on the debate, but it will remain approximate, imperfect, and always ethereal.

We need to face it: An absolute agreement on value may not be possible, and therefore the same is true about price. This is why we have markets and central exchanges to *discover* price. In other words, find the *estimated* or *expected* value behind the price to enable exchange. This is what happens when market participants quote (in the pit, on the phone, or on screen) back and forth. They are responding and competing to get the price they desire as new information and needs enter the market. With this dance of price discovery, a symbolic numerical record of points of transactions is left in its trail and a pattern is revealed showing a quantitative record of human reactions to the ongoing influences behind it. The resulting pattern is a visual of the structure of prices, recording the needs of the market players, their sentiments, anticipations, and actions.

Quantifying the Unquantifiable

I think it is clearly inherently impossible to ever know what value is and agree on price. Yet the dynamics of price expression are observed and modeled by legions of physicists, engineers, quantitative mathematicians, and even code-breaking cryptographers, each looking for any hint of information with predictive value, something to point us to the future direction of the price. As trading becomes more and more automatic and digitized, our conception of price further changes. With quantitative analysis tools and the automation of rapid trading, we have started to concentrate more on the symbolic abstraction of price and less on what drives the actual exchange. This abstraction risks removing ourselves from the significance of the price.

Could it be that our own current and ever-elaborate methods lead us to ask the wrong questions? That our methods may even adopt the wrong metrics—metrics that have little basis in the reality of today's markets? What, for example, is the logic of buying if a price goes above the 200-day moving average? Sure, this will put you into a market that has been trending up and may continue to do so (or not), but other than the logic of linear mathematics, what is the relationship of a 200-day progression of price to the underlying market?

Traders act within this model even though they know that markets are driven by human reaction. As traders, we act on emotions, yet the human sensibilities of market participants are given relatively little consideration in most price analysis. Is it because we simply cannot quantify the ethereal? Is it as Benoit Mandelbrot says? He states: "It is psychology, individual and mass—even harder to fathom than the paradoxes of quantum mechanics. Anticipation is the stuff of dreams and vapors."[1]

The answer may be simple. We are quite possibly using incomplete metrics to quantify something that cannot be quantified with the tools we use. It could be that our instinctive drive for precision and order is defeating our quest for an order that does not innately exist. The recent crisis in the credit and banking industries will be a case study for decades. In these examples, we saw derivative products such as collateralized debt obligations (CDOs) and markets for them created where it was simply not possible to logically price them based on any previous experience—nor did it matter. A tool from another domain was simply applied to making prices for CDOs—a model based on the statistical correlations determined by a Gaussian copula—and, with this, a perceived order was imposed on a constructed market.[2] Voila! A price could be quoted for CDOs. In short, the ability for pricing (regardless of *how* a price was created), enabled a perception of order, exchange, and gave the sense of a real market—creating with it a new reality and perhaps a truly ethereal market (little different from the windmills in Don Quixote's mind in this chapter's opening quote).

Markets created to "offset risk" without a pricing mechanism based in the realities of Econ 101 (the most basic lessons of economics) increased risk in an ever-expanding systemic market with therefore exploding systemic risk. The most fundamental question (What is the price?) was not understood, even with the most sophisticated mathematics. An absolute faith in quantitative pricing models (a logical development from the Efficient Market Hypothesis (EMH) that entered the economic canon of accepted thought in the 1960s and 1970s) could quite possibly be the culprit.

The Trader's Dissonance: Control over Uncertainties, Action, and Consensus

The trader's dissonance is that we are working with imperfections—from units of pricing, to information, to our own perceptions and varied analysis. Pricing is ultimately an abstract symbolization of an exchange between two parties. The information behind the exchange can be flawed, is almost never complete, and is sometimes downright deceptive, and perception is always subjective. Out of this mix we create analyses and act on decisions based on the analyses, but we will never have perfect results, understanding, or complete truth. To expect anything other than this may be our first logical error. So, how do we cope? We create tools and models and metrics of understanding in an attempt to capture repeatable results. We do this because, as discussed earlier, human nature is such that we are extremely uncomfortable with uncertainties. Uncertainty can cause distress and dysfunction. So to handle that, we use tools of certainty (absolute quantitative models) to impose a sense of order (real or not) and apply perceived certainties onto the markets. This makes us feel more secure. We do this by quantifying the details of vast reams of data of price history and production to give us answers so we can confidently take action.

Our need for order may be behind the great appeal of the Efficient Market Hypothesis, generally accepted and adopted in recent decades. EMH contends that all relevant information is known and instantly priced, ergo it is efficient. Further, it also holds that the efficient market will immediately absorb and react to new information. Price reflects this and is always correct. Contrary to the hypothesis, we can ask this question: If markets deliver efficient prices, then why do we trade? Why would one speculate on future value?

Sophisticated methods of market analysis took off only in the late 1970s and with it EMH. Richard Thaler cites that in the 1980s economist Marc Reinganum asserted, concerning the observation of ongoing seasonality in equity markets,

> *What then do the anomalies mean? They mean that the most interesting insights into the pricing behavior of stocks are being discovered by tedious and painstakingly thorough examination of data. That means that, in the constant ebb and flow between theory and empirics, empirics currently holds the upper hand. In other words, systematic quantification of reams of data would give us the answers, show the way.*[3]

Thaler then countered this in the early 1990s:

> I do not agree . . . the clues that will allow us to understand the puzzles must come from additional econometric and experimental investigations. Only then can the formal modelers try to put the pieces together conceptually. The challenge, then, is really to all economists to try to understand why the seasonal price movements occur. And how they can persist for at least 90 years and for at least 50 years after their existence has been published.[4]

Given the direction of this discussion over the past 30 or 40 years, and real market developments, we may now be entering a phase where the behavioral economists will have the upper hand.

Trading Triggers

Robert Olsen states:

> . . . to make a decision, emotion is the necessary trigger [and] without emotion, one would be reduced to the state of an idiot savant who goes on endlessly calculating without the ability to make a choice.[5]

I suspect that what Olsen and his colleagues in behavioral finance mean by the preceding statement is that endless calculations on the abstraction of price (price being a symbolic abstraction of the underlying transaction) reduce the market participant to the "idiot savant"—one with no emotion or deeper understanding of what "it" is.

To buy or sell is a decision and this holds a thought, idea, and expectation behind it—an emotion to trigger the decision. Often the dominant forces behind the prices are not considered and maybe not even comprehended.

When there are unnatural conditions or made-up (artificial) forces dominating a market (as in the U.S. housing and related markets of the past few years), the natural price-discovery process is silenced. True price is quashed and a setup for drastic change is in the making. The natural forces will line up to assert themselves in the pricing mechanism of an open market, resulting in change and opportunity.

The much-recounted blowup of LTCM discussed in the previous chapter, and its play into the pricing of some markets (but most importantly interest rates at the time), is the best-documented and most well-known episode of this. The forces at play in the U.S. housing and related markets are still unfolding and financial history is in the making. (In subsequent chapters, we will look at the dynamics of "unnatural forces" and "animal spirits" in familiar markets and how they can be detected for trading opportunities in patterns and price behavior.)

Sentiment and Consensus

In trading, we take many things into account when deciding to make a transaction. We can agree that the current price reflects a certain sentiment and consensus. These two ideas give us a sense of order when evaluating a market such as that for homebuyers when considering recent sales of similar properties. Additionally, there are now increasing attempts to measure and understand market sentiment and consensus in order to be ahead of the crowd.

Consensus is a state residing in a common belief system. A state of consensus is one where we share the same reference points, set of values, and sources of information. Consensus drives the group to which one belongs. So price, then, does not really reflect efficiencies but rather the group or herding behavior of the "dominant tribe." When market participants find consensus, often what is happening is that the price is not efficient but simply reflects the dominant group's *sentiment* (the loudest message and strongest emotional reactions to the consensus-created message). Behavioral economists are now demonstrating that price movements are often related to custom, to what we believe, and to the habits of the participants in our group. Perhaps John Maynard Keynes said it best in his opus magnum, *General Theory of Employment, Interest, and Money* when he claimed that most investors' decisions are merely the result of "animal spirits."

In any case, consensus is a driver of price. And as participants in a tribe, we are focused on the dominant members of and influences on our herd and tend to miss the less-dominant, or not-yet-dominant, groups. We often do not see the fringes of the other herd(s) portending the next direction and change. We are too busy among ourselves, with our tribe/group, and with our own consensus. But to see where we may be going next, the challenge for the speculator is to understand the active forces at play—even on the fringe of activity—to detect why and when the dominant tribe weakens and spot the emerging tribes. Then we can attempt to anticipate the future.

WHAT DRIVES THE HERD?   The "thundering herd" (reminiscent of the terrific Merrill Lynch ad of the late 1970s with the herd of bull cattle thundering across the Great Plains) is an apt expression describing a computer science phenomenon called the *thundering herd problem*. It happens when a large number of competing processes gather. While gathered, they await an event to trigger processing. Because only one process can proceed (or execute) at a time, there is a struggle over "who" goes first, or "who" gets the price. The members of the herd (or, the processes) wake up and all fight over the same resource to execute. This moment of awakening is brief and violent, like the spooking of a herd of cattle. Just as in a collective market of traders, a decision is made as to which processes (or, prevailing group sentiment) can continue or dominate the direction. When this happens, a direction emerges until buyers and sellers are satisfied, and, just as in the computer world, the remaining processes (or, price competitors) are put back to sleep. In addition, like the computer processes, the market then reaches equilibrium and continues again to quietly forage for opportunity.

Each player (or group) goes about its business, waiting for the next impulse to trigger an event and elicit an emotional impulse to make an exchange. We, of course, can see that it is more efficient if only one process is awoken at a time but this is not how it happens in reality. In the markets there is a struggle and competition to execute. When there are no disturbances or new bits of information, the herd will appear inactive. (We experience "sleepy" markets.) But, inevitably, all participants will wake up to compete for access to the resource when an impulse is triggered. Then, the participants of the dominant tribe (those with the strongest consensus) will be the ones to execute transactions and drive the direction (or trend) of the market.

We are all bombarded with messages, advice, and expert knowledge on every aspect of life, including the markets. This input is what feeds the tribe and creates the consensus. Yet, as we sometimes learn, a message can be incomplete, a distraction, or even deceptive. (And when it is framed within credibility, the truth is even more difficult to decipher.) This is where the dynamics of consensus are at work on price. At some point, however, truth in price will prevail. It always does. Meanwhile, groups are subject to enormous spells of assumptions based on expectations, and overall irrationality sometimes makes them respond to the emotions *around the message* instead of the facts. This happens because when a message appeals to emotion, we tend to displace facts out of plain sight and become blinded (as we saw in the anecdotes of Chapter 1; we will also see this dynamic at play in price patterns in the following chapters).

Many times, if the facts are too difficult to accept, too complicated, or even too painful, our emotions naturally kick in to take over and guide us. We ask ourselves what will make us *feel* better, no matter how much good information we have at our disposal or how great the brains behind the analysis in front of us. Ultimately, when emotions are feeding the tribe, a defining pattern emerges; we have a setup of conditions and see the patterns of the dominant tribe at work.

THE HERD AND ITS TRIBES MAKE THE MARKET Figure 2.1 illustrates tribes (groups of stocks) moving independently of each other. Some of the tribes are large and some are small, but each is seeking opportunity and perceived value in search of the right price. This is what we and the markets do when conditions are not threatening and there is a perception of safety.

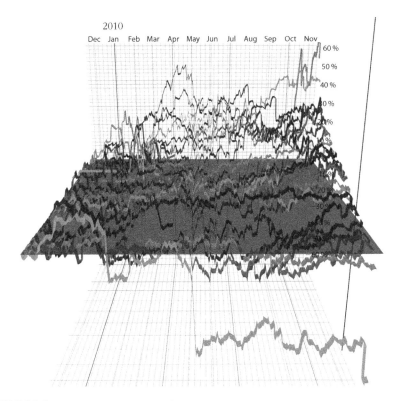

FIGURE 2.1 Independent Tribes without a Dominant Force
Source: www.Metaview.tv

The orderly search for value among the tribes and their members is taking place in Figure 2.1. Under these conditions, tribes are not threatened by each other, nor is there any discord. A climate of foraging and opportunism reigns. It is a market in balance and is a "normal" state. Inevitably this will change. It rarely lasts long and detecting the shift will spell opportunity for the trader.

The shift begins when a competing consensus, for an individual equity or the entire market, starts to build and a new dominant tribe emerges. In the shift's early phases, participants may be at opposite ends of the consensus price. Here, a struggle between tribes takes place as the market shift starts to kick in. Because no single force or tribe can maintain dominance, one tribe will always be replaced by another. A telltale sign of a consensus shift is, for example, a pickup in volatility or rate of change. The greater the struggle, the more violent (i.e., volatile) the price range may be as the consensus competes to arrive at a new direction. The macro-dynamic of the thundering herd problem in the marketplace is in force. To capture this similar dynamic and in recent years, State Street Corporation, for example, has been working on developing behavior measures to capture investor flows into various assets and sectors. To this end, the Turbulence Index[6] was developed to help identify shifts and tipping points of change.

If we were to plot price of an active market over a longer time, we would see an extended curve, representing a larger and enduring struggle, one with strong emotions in the market at times of change. During change and with a new and emerging tribe, the market's behavioral characteristics include conflicting sentiment, and confusion among and within tribes (the market players), deception, and bouts of extreme volatility.

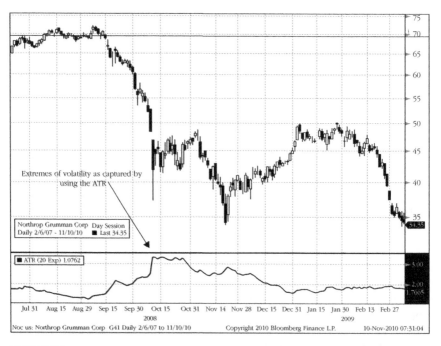

FIGURE 2.2 Northrop Gruman Corp. Daily: Volatity Extreme and Market Struggle.
Source: Copyright 2010 Bloomberg Finance LP.

Option strategies (a topic outside the scope of this book) is where the actual or implied volatility of price is traded in an attempt to profit from rapid shift of dominance, and the resulting market condition shown in

Figure 2.2 where there is a peak in volatility. [Volatility here is measured by the 20-period *average true range (ATR)* calculation developed by Wells Wilder to measure price volatility.]

THE LOCKSTEP MARCH OF PRICE   What happens when a tribe and its members each stops seeking value? When they are not even motivated by value? What happens when there are no enemies or competitors, when there is no dominant tribe and all move in concert as a single herd? This happens when neither opportunity nor constructs of value are even considered. Price is driven by emotions. A lockstep in price is a result of fear driving the participants. For example, with prices accelerating to the upside, there is a fear of failing to execute or to get your price. Participants then chase the trade as the price marches upward. To the downside, each tribe and each participant searches for safety and shelter, or to get out of the market. Investors and traders are no longer responding to fundamentals. Information on balance sheets and earnings is ignored. It is more commonly called a "market crisis" as pricing to value completely disappears (which may present an extreme opportunity). These dynamics are shown in the three-dimensional (3-D) visualization product, Metaview, as well as other, two-dimensional visualization tools supplied by various analysis programs.

Whether locked tightly in a flow of dominant tribes or in the thundering herd, tribes and their members feed off the information in a signal loop to create a lockstep. Tribes and their members watch what the others are doing. The market takes on a lockstep pattern (which is now a herd moving) and begins to move in unison (see Figure 2.3). Each tribe or member seeks to be part of the entire movement for both the survival of the herd and their own survival.

No matter the overall direction, when the lockstep pattern to the upside or downside is in place, we have the first condition leading to the inevitable signal of a *shift away* from the lockstep. Timing is exceedingly difficult and thought to be a factor of luck and good intuition. Yet, with pattern recognition techniques we can identify the indicators of a shift from the lockstep market condition. This happens when, for example, the first tribes begin to break away from the herd. Signs of opportunistic behavior among the few emerge, signaling the end of the lockstep move.

The market conditions in Figure 2.4 powerfully illustrate the signal with a very large brush illustrating concepts of how behavior dynamics can drive price. This is the backdrop of our interest in unfolding patterns of price behavior and the information they give us. It is the reason why we need to adjust our mindset and why we seek predictive significance to price patterns. Then, we can apply this to a trading strategy. But first, here are some thoughts about endeavors in prediction.

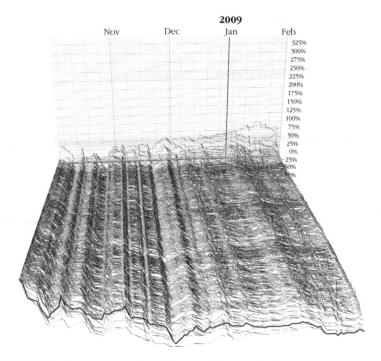

FIGURE 2.3 Visual Representation of Entire Market and All Groups/Tribes Moving in Lockstep

Source: www.Metaview.tv.

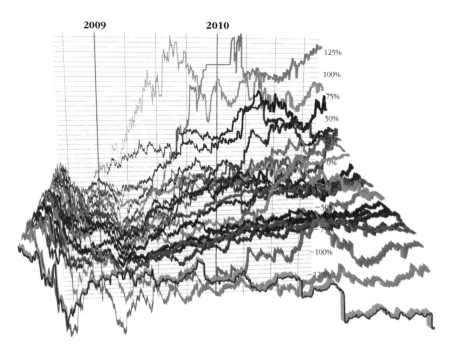

FIGURE 2.4 Breaking Away from the Herd in Early 2009.

Source: www.Metaview.tv.

Prediction

One can say that reliable prediction is impossible. That is mostly correct, but perhaps also irrelevant. In trading, being "right" and "winning" as a market participant is not the same as in sports, or in most commercial endeavors. So, is there folly in trying to forecast? Yes and no. The industry pays legions of very smart people to forecast future events, probabilities, and price: from the size of a corn crop and its expected price at harvest, to weather, to survival rates in population groups. Our economy and society depend on forecasting to make decisions as to where and how to allocate resources.

Forecasts are never exact but remain a helpful guide to value and price within a particular context. For us, the core (but surely not the only) idea of speculating on price direction is that the best indicator of prices to come is the emerging pattern of price right now. Without debunking price forecasting, getting oneself caught up in price projections may be self-defeating. Yet in spite of that, we continue to conduct this exercise as it gives us a sense of control over our surroundings and aids in decision making and resource allocation. We simply need to forecast.

However, traders do not forecast with certainty. (That is the work of analysts, who help provide the *hows* and *whys* of price direction.) Why is this so? State a price target and we lose our objectivity. We risk concerning ourselves with the objective and not with the realities of the current price action. We project our expectations (hopes) onto managing the trade, and become focused on the abstract price (often determined by esoteric mathematical methods that might have little logic or basis in the underlying market) instead of the message of the actual price action in front of us. Instead of seeing, we start to *anticipate* and *hope*. We impose our own ego on the vision of the market instead of allowing the market to show us. When this happens, we become blind and need to find a way back to the core truths behind the price action. We can do this by sharpening our recognition of patterns and resulting price rather than forecasting price.

Tools to Recognize Patterns

Visualization of price started with the first group of "chartists." Those first price charts are a little different from the elaborate and highly developed tools of data visualization we use today. Conceptually, they are the same. Yet those first equity price charts were a breakthrough in representing price history. When chartists plotted price data onto sheets of graph paper, patterns emerged and previously undetected information was immediately revealed. This is the essence of technical analysis of price.

Thinking about it now, it is hard to imagine that charts as we know them (even the candlestick charts from the mid-18th century that were

introduced to the Western trading community only about 25 years ago)
are a recent innovation. The first bar charts were used around the time
syndicates were said to control much of the price action, in the late 19th
and early 20th centuries. Reliable information and reporting was difficult, if
not impossible, to locate. Yet price and volume were available to all. So, a
few creative "little guys" started plotting prices onto graph paper and began
to detect patterns with telltale traces of what we call *buying and selling
support; tops, bottoms,* and *wedges;* and *breakouts of flags and pennants.*
Patterns of price congestion, reversals, and support; wide or narrow ranges
of buying and selling—all this information was revealed through patterns.
Then, Charles Dow (founder of the Dow Jones Average and the *Wall Street
Journal*) went a step further with the creation of *point and fig*ure charts.

The language of chart analysis is still used today well over 100 years
later. In spite of the skepticism of the chartists even back then, much of the
same methods they pioneered remain with us today. The essential metric,
or set of data—price—then time (and some would say volume) remain the
core of decision making and price patterns.

Data is reduced to a single input—the raw input of price. Now, as
visualization possibilities become ever-more elaborate and expressive of the
underlying price information, there are growing capabilities to represent price
beyond the traditional charting methods with which we are all familiar—
for example, a 3-D representation of price, or maybe with a frequency
overlay along with the transaction source.

The charts that most traders work with (and those in this book) use
a linear dimension with a horizontal showing the time relationship and a
vertical showing the numerical relationship. This puts price in context over
time. Figure 2.5, however, shows a snapshot of more information, using
"heat maps."

A heat map is a graphical representation of data—X,Y, and value, with
the values shown in hues of different colors to tell us about density or
degree. Currently, with massive computer power and a flood of accessible
information, we are on the cusp of heralding a leap in market visualization
of price and information through improvements of tools like heat maps.
Future innovations in charting will give us greater discreteness in pattern
recognition and increased ability to make associations of information from the
patterns of price and additional related information.

Another example of an emerging method of visualization to rapidly
detect relationships and changes is the "Bubble Map" shown in Figure 2.6.

These developments are similar to the leap of predictive visual analysis
developed by the early chartist, Homma, of Osaka, Japan, in the late 18th
century, or Charles Dow. We now have the visualization tools to overlay
information from news, liquidity sources, and order size onto charts to
reveal information and data relationships not previously detected. With
the emerging visualization technologies of the near future, we may be

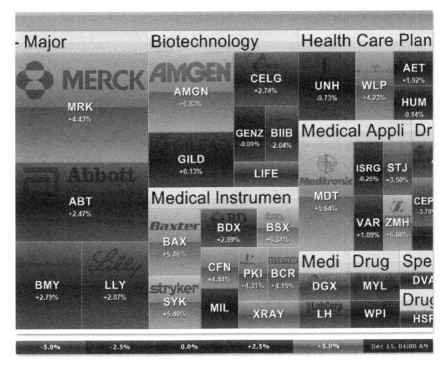

FIGURE 2.5 Market Heat Map
Source: www.finviz.com.

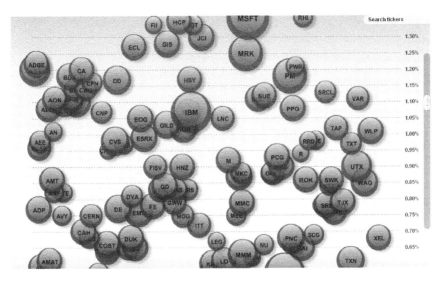

FIGURE 2.6 Market Bubble Map
Source: www.finviz.com.

able to include metrics on things previously thought of as intangibles and difficult to pinpoint, such as sentiment risk, market optimism, expectation, and anticipation. Technologies like these would allow us, for example, to immediately identify the dynamics driving the dominant tribe, or to see degrees of herding behavior or emerging influences before the market shifts to a new direction.

Conclusion

With objective tools used in pattern recognition, we will be able to see and act on ever-changing markets rather than relying on static methods of prediction. To build and use our tools, we must be alert to influences, many with the power to blind us. These blinding influences include our instinct to join a group and move with, and by, consensus; the potential folly and mental trappings of relying solely on static predictions; and the tendency to imagine treacherous forces out to derail us from our victories in the affairs of the market. When the only devious forces working against us are more like the windmills in *Don Quixote*: They are of our own making and in our own minds. Many times, *we alone* prevent ourselves from seeing the message in front of us.

In the face of these influences, in the next chapters we will look at some basic and practical approaches to recognition of the patterns of price behavior, and discover why certain and simple methods can help us make sense of what the market is telling us and to guide our trading.

CHAPTER 3

An Upside Reversal

"If I remember right" Sancho replied, "I've already asked you once or twice not to correct my words if you don't understand what I mean by them—and if you don't understand, you can always say, 'Sancho, you devil, I don't understand you,' and if I still don't make my meaning clear you can correct me, because I'm so practible . . ."

"I don't understand you, Sancho," Don Quixote interrupted, "I don't know what 'I'm so practible' means.

"'So practible,'" Sancho replied, "means that's just the way I am."

"And now I understand you even less," Don Quixote replied.

"If you don't understand me," Sancho replied, "I don't know what else to say—that's all I do know, so help me god."

"What you intend to say is that you're so tractable, pliant and docile that you will accept everything I say, and learn whatever I teach you."

"I bet," said Sancho, "you knew exactly what I meant from the start, but you wanted to ruffle me so as to make me put my foot in it another few hundred times."

—The Ingenious Hidalgo Don Quixote de la Mancha
by Miguel de Cervantes Saavedra.
[Translated by John Rutherford, Penguin Books,
London (2003), p. 527.]

This chapter looks at some of the most basic concepts and market patterns used in pattern recognition, starting with a look at the keystone of all patterns—support and resistance. However, before we do that, we'll step away from the abstract of the previous chapters and think about the simple and practical expressions we use in market pattern recognition.

Decidedly, some of the language used in trading and for descriptions of unfolding patterns sounds quite unscientific. We use expressions like "abandoned baby" or "three black birds" to describe candlestick chart patterns or "jumping the creek" to explain patterns behind Wyckoff analysis. All of these expressions are actually quite efficient in describing the rich visual patterns in our charts. Using concepts familiar to us in the everyday world to describe a pattern is often the best way to express what is sometimes quite complex.

We will start with the idea and pattern of *support* and *resistance (S&R)*, familiar to most readers, and from this progress to our patterns "knock on the door," the "snake," the "coil," and the "ambush." In later chapters we will talk about our "Adam and Eve" pattern, for example, built on elements of the basic patterns of snake and coil. First, we examine the keystone pattern of S&R.

Borders of Price: Support and Resistance

Anyone with the most cursory interest in technical analysis is acquainted with ideas of support and resistance. And even if you have looked at only a few charts of linear price progression, you've probably identified repeated clusters of exchange, which mark a clearly defined price range. If we have experience with this, we might think we know exactly what is meant by support and resistance. Yet it is when we think we have a complete understanding of something and then take the time to revisit the basic idea—regardless of the field of endeavor—that we best understand the more complex ideas that are built on the seemingly simple concepts.

An absolute handle on support and resistance will help us easily recognize some of the more complex patterns all markets reveal to us every day. An analogy could be, for example, when one can immediately identify a diamond by recognizing the most basic and defining characteristics of a raw diamond in the sludge.

Not to be confused with *trend-line support and resistance*, support is the price range over time where buying appears to come into the market. Its counter is resistance, where price is rejected and met with selling. The interplay between support and resistance is the foundation of many patterns and trading strategies. What, then, does the conceptual pattern of support and resistance look like?

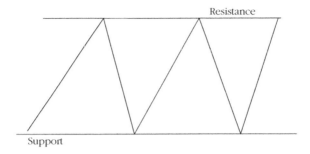

FIGURE 3.1 Simple Concept of Support and Resistance

Looking at Figure 3.1, we can ask: Why do markets seem to cluster around price points, or return to "old" prices? What is the logic behind this seemingly simplistic concept of technical analysis? Is the idea of supporting prices and resisting prices nothing more than techno-babble? I think not; price is a metric of action by market participants. There is reason and purpose behind our actions and therefore a reason for the points illustrated in Figure 3.1.

In liquid markets, with diverse participants and motivations, price remains in constant motion in the search for value. A metaphor would be pools of water in grassy savannahs driven by rain, changing water tables, and vegetation; the pools are in continuous flux as they seek their lowest level. They will meet support and resistance at the borders of the closed, but changing, natural system. Driven by changing influences and information, price, too, is in constant movement as it seeks value.

As in our savannah, without new information or a disturbance to drive new and dominating motivations in the markets, price will oscillate in a range as it seeks value in this closed system we call the *marketplace.* Attempts by the collective value-seeking market to carry a financial instrument outside the true value range will always be met with buying (if value is perceived) or selling (when price is rejected by market participants).

Do markets have memory? Like the people behind the markets, yes, they do. And markets, like all natural systems (including human systems), tend to repeat behavior. While we are never absolutely predictable, human motivations change little, if at all, over time. On a personal note, I've observed it in myself in something ordinary. In the fall, I like to buy seasonal products at the farmer's market. Come early October, I may go from stand to stand looking for the best price. All seem to be the same, with little variation. However, the prices can drastically change from year to year, depending on how plentiful the yield—which was dependent on the condition of the soil and summer rains. In any given year fruit can become very expensive relative to other years. When this happens, I might hesitate and buy just a few fruits, or just not buy any at all. This could be likened to my price rejection and repeated behavior at the top of the range, or as price entered new higher levels. If not enough buyers emerge to absorb the sparse yield at the price I've also rejected, prices will drop to where buying can be found and merchants will move what is left of their seasonal yield. At that point, support is found.

When I go back to the market the next year, I might wander over to a stand and spot a price much lower than last year and think, "I don't remember seeing prices this low for years." So, I join other buyers and freely buy. The price is familiar. It was established before and acts as *perceived value*. This is *price memory*, acceptance by the market, and is support. You can observe this behavior in yourself next time you buy products where the price fluctuates from season to season. Figure 3.1 is nothing more than a conceptual illustration of the farmer's market example of support and resistance, and market memory. With this in mind, you can ask yourself how the concept of support and resistance exhibits itself in real-life, familiar market examples.

Beyond the Borders of Price

In the broader liquid markets, price moving within borders of price tells us we have a market in equilibrium and seeking value, as shown in Figures 3.2, 3.3, and 3.4. Again, this is not too different from the previous example of the pools of water moving in steady equilibrium trying to find the lowest level in a somewhat closed ecosystem. Things remain this way until there is a disturbance or a change to the system.

Looking at the figures, the idea seems quite simple. Traditional trading strategies built on trend-following methods enter positions on a breakout of a defined support-and-resistance range. Patterns of breakouts from a support-and-resistance channel can be easily identified by both visual and numerical methods, and therefore is an attractive tool for adopting trading strategies and creating mechanical trading systems. An attempt to "trade the breakout" may be quantified with the program script using the following code script logic:

```
HPoint = highest high over the last n days (as of yesterday)
LPoint = lowest low over the last n days (as of yesterday)
     P = today's price (i.e., the close)
   if P > HPoint then
             Buy
else if P < LPoint then
           Sell
           end
```

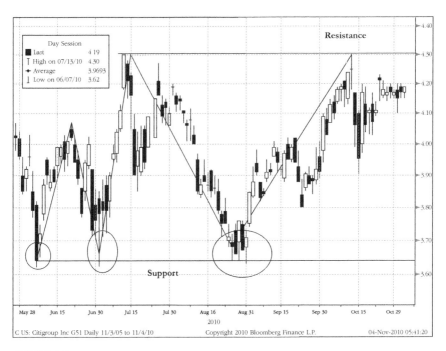

FIGURE 3.2 Citigroup, Inc. Daily: Support and Resistance Range
Source: Copyright 2010 Bloomberg Finance LP.

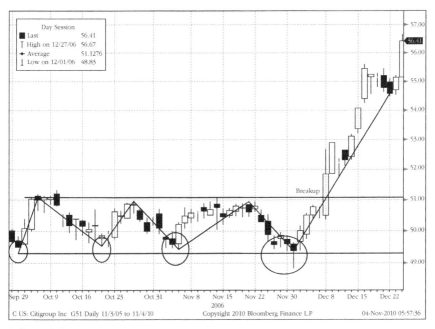

FIGURE 3.3 Citigroup, Inc. Daily: Breakout of Support and Resistance
Source: Copyright 2010 Bloomberg Finance LP.

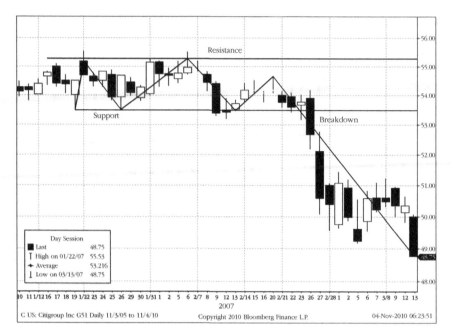

FIGURE 3.4 Citigroup Daily: Breakdown from Support and Resistance
Source: Copyright 2010 Bloomberg Finance LP.

An illustration of the price action that this script logic would capture is shown in Figures 3.3 and 3.4.

While this script is based on the ideas of support and resistance, it is not built on the ideas of pattern recognition. Instead, it is based on measurements of a new price range over a specific period of time. The script, however, is unable to capture everything. Critical visual information is lost. Observation of the characteristics of the price range and overall market behavior are not relevant to the method and not considered here. Only time and numerical price are considered. The mechanical rule-based approach in the program script is unable to capture information the market may convey within the patterns.

Predictive Price Action within the Price Channel: Hearing Music through the Market Noise

Within the support and resistance (S&R) band there is something characterized as "market noise." This is the granular, subtle, and telling detail of price action in a shorter time scale. Unlike the background noise surrounding us at a football game (the sounds of the crowd not related to the plays on the field, for instance), this noise tells us much about the condition of price action and where it could be headed. It delivers predictive information to the trader. And in the event of a breakout captured by our eye, instinct, experience, or mechanical rules, understanding the noise leading up to a game-changing market shift (or price breakout) helps us flush out the pretender from the real deal.

What is a trend? This is a philosophical question that can lead to larger discussions. For purposes of this book, we will keep it simple and confine it to visually identifying and connecting points of higher highs (met by price rejection and selling) and points of lower lows (met with price rejection and buying). We will look at these trend channels within considered borders of support and resistance.

Figure 3.5 shows a trend-line connecting at least two points and captures the third swing down. Spotting and identifying a trend channel like this within a larger pattern of support and resistance is the *granular* feature of a pattern constellation. Price behavior patterns like this within the keystones of S&R can be critical bits of information. But do markets always behave just as they appear in Figure 3.5? No, never exactly. But as we will see, they do display distinctive and defining features that we can easily visually capture.

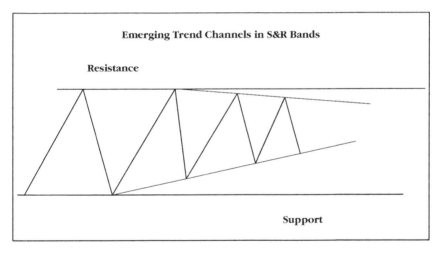

FIGURE 3.5 Emerging Trend Channels within S&R Bands

The trend-lines shown in Figures 3.5 and 3.6 are a conceptual guide not only for possible trade entry or exit, but also help us identify the dynamics of a much larger pattern that might be unfolding. (We will come back to this idea on trading tactics in Chapters 6 through 8.) Here, the pattern behavior we see within S&R could be a possible signal of an emerging market shift, a breakup in the direction of the herd or emerging dominant tribe (discussed in Chapter 2), which appears on the larger surface to be still moving in equilibrium.

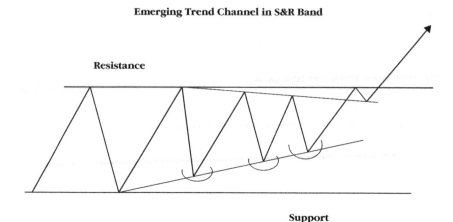

Emerging Trend Channel in S&R Band

Resistance

Support

FIGURE 3.6 Emerging Trend Channel and Dynamics within S&R Bands

Let's concentrate on the two real-life granular patterns within the indentified band of S&R: trend action and the minor and major support levels. These ideas are familiar to most of us. In the real world, traders come into contact with something much more complex unfolding within any defined price band than the theoretical straight-line example in Figure 3.6, which illustrates the pattern of identified support levels that are now moving up within the band.

First, what can we pinpoint as the conditions of this theoretical market?

1. We have a defined price band between the S&R lines.
2. Within the band, we observe (with the use of very simple trend channel analysis techniques) emerging buying pressure. Some may take volume into consideration behind these patterns to see if this buying pressure is supported by volume. But, to focus, we will take a purist approach and rely on the idea that the price pattern alone is enough information for pattern analysis and trade decision.

And what would be the conditions of such a scenario in the real markets? See Figure 3.7.

Figure 3.7 points to a potential violation to the upside within the S&R. We have price breaking a trend-line to the upside within the S&R band, and then returning to kiss the internal violated trend-line (a pattern component we will further discuss in Chapter 4) and closing the gap within the S&R band. With this work done, there follows a decisive break out of the S&R range.

As a result of this, the previous resistance becomes the new support. Again, this is a conceptual dynamic of the pattern. We see in the weekly

FIGURE 3.7 Fuel Systems Solutions Inc., Daily
Source: Copyright 2010 Bloomberg Finance LP.

FIGURE 3.8 TEVA Pharmaceutical Industries Ltd., Weekly
Source: Copyright 2010 Bloomberg Finance LP.

TEVA chart in Figure 3.8 that after the first breakout of the resistance range, the market returned into the price channel to close price gaps at major support of the time at 70.00. This interplay of price pattern is a tenet of visual price analysis and can also be seen in Figure 3.9.

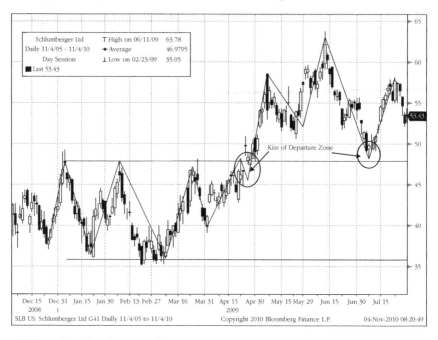

FIGURE 3.9 Schlumberger Ltd., Daily
Source: Copyright 2010 Bloomberg Finance LP.

What We See (and Why We See It)

For the careful observer, the breakout of a price resistance range might not be interpreted as a breakout or a trade to take, even when every mechanical system is ringing the buy signals over your speakers.

Let's take two traders, A and B. For Trader A, support ranges are buying opportunities. These same ranges are ignored by Trader B. Why? We can think back to our hiking example from Chapter 1, where we had two people with the same pattern of weather information in front of them, yet each of them perceived the reality of what came next against a completely different set of experiences and expectations. Just as they saw the information in front of them differently, so will the ranges we're discussing be considered by one trader and ignored by the other. We cannot say exactly whether one trader is right and the other wrong, but only that their experience, and the rules and habits of their individual observations, gave them different answers; it is no different with price observation. The greater our set of real-world experiences, the better we see and understand and the more skilled we are.

And there is more. A pattern in isolation tells only part of the unfolding story of price action. Trading a classic textbook description of a breakout while ignoring the internals or granularity of price behavior and information around the breakout can (and often does) lead us into chasing one false breakout after another. What distinguishes a real opportunity from a false one may be in the small but essential characteristics of the developing pattern. We will see, too, that it is also the context of the pattern in relation to a surrounding pattern unfolding over time—including background sentiment and information leaking into the market—that will influence the actions of the dominant tribe of the market herd and price direction.

Differentiating the Real Deal from the Pretenders

What started out as a discussion of a basic foundation of pattern analysis with S&R has quickly taken on more complexity as the preceding figures and examples show; they might now raise more questions than they answer.

For example, Figure 3.10 is an illustration of a trend channel within S&R, with a resistance breakout to revisit previous resistance, reject price, and move

FIGURE 3.10 iShares Global Materials Sector Index Fund, Daily
Source: Copyright 2010 Bloomberg Finance LP.

up. We can identify something else emerging *within* the S&R: the internal price pattern that predicted a likely breakout. Understanding price action within support and resistance and spotting an emerging trend channel where the market is doing most of its work of price discovery helps us detect a possible trend shift and reversal. With this, our observation and analysis go beyond concentrating on the static range of identified support and resistance (as in the pseudo script code above) to an examination of the price action within.

When is a reversal in price real and when is it fake? When is it simply noise, or, better yet, noise with a message? Of course, we know for sure only after the fact.

Let's look at the three S&R ranges shown in Figures 3.11, 3.12, 3.13, and 3.14. One of these examples prove to be the real deal and two are pretenders. As with anything else in life, when we understand even the most banal details very well, we can immediately spot the phony from the genuine article. Can you spot the telltale and subtle characteristics alerting us to the pretenders in the room?

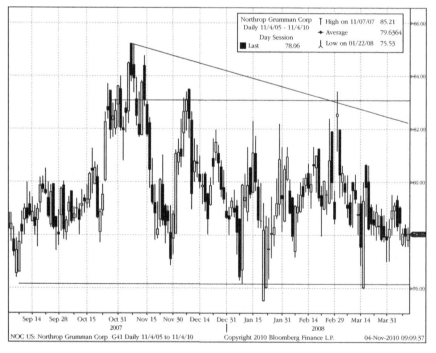

FIGURE 3.11 Northrop Grumman, Corp., Daily
Source: Copyright 2010 Bloomberg Finance LP.

If you can't yet tell from your experience and these few visuals of S&R or emerging trend channels within S&R, we will come back to these patterns and be able to immediately spot the pretenders. You may also want

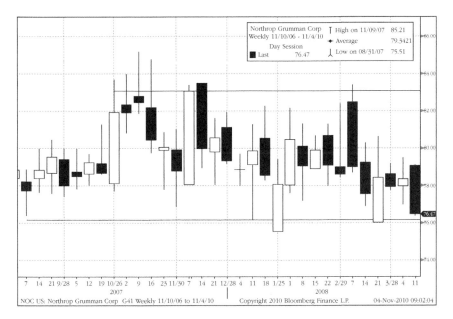

FIGURE 3.12 Northrop Grumman, Corp., Weekly
Source: Copyright 2010 Bloomberg Finance LP.

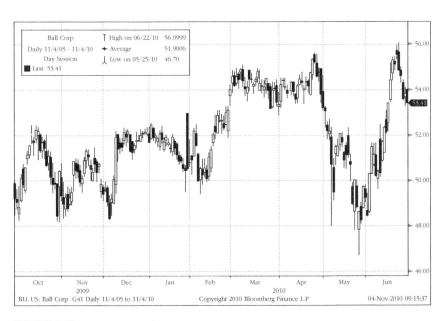

FIGURE 3.13 Ball Corp., Daily
Source: Copyright 2010 Bloomberg Finance LP.

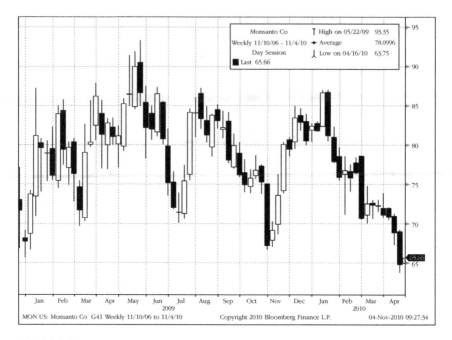

FIGURE 3.14 Monsanto, Weekly
Source: Copyright 2010 Bloomberg Finance LP.

to review a daily chart of Monsanto (MON) from January 2009. But first, let's review some of the pattern features that can lead us to the real deal.

Knock on the Door

Often, the sustained breakout announces itself by *knocking on the door* before jumping into the room. We see this from both large, multiyear trends and micro-intraday trends. Unlike the pretender, the real-deal guest doesn't suddenly blast through the door and into your living room, but politely announces itself with a ring of the bell or a knock on the door. Readers of literature can think of this as similar to *foreshadowing*—where a future event is subtly indicated or predicted by what may seem an insignificant detail of the story. Markets often display this price pattern behavior.

At times, and in the more liquid markets, price action will foreshadow a significant move on the horizon. This subtle pattern tends to be overlooked by traders and attributed to noise or what is known as *short covering* (traders buying back what was "sold short" at first). However, just as in literary foreshadowing there is a predictive message behind the noise. And it is a pattern we can see in multiple time frames.

This knock on the door should not be confused with what traders like to refer to as the "dead cat bounce" (a price bounce seen during an accelerated downtrend). Unlike the dead cat bounce, the knock must break significant trend price points as defined by either a trend-line or key resistance line violation. This idea is illustrated in Figure 3.15.

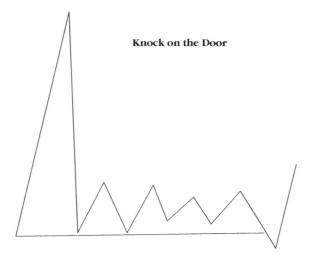

FIGURE 3.15 Knock on the Door Concept

Many of us remember the surprising and brief events of the Gold market in late 1999. Currently, we are in the midst of a long-term bull Gold market that kicked off in the year 2000. What were the triggers for this bull market move, this knock on the door? Gold was in a long-term price decline since the early 1980s. In the spring of 1999, the British Treasury announced continued plans to unload more of its reserves, as central banks had been doing over the past years. On July 6, 1999, the market herd reacted to this information by selling, and the front month futures contract subsequently settled at a 20-year low of $257.80 an ounce. With this, the downward trend accelerated.

A few months later, in September 1999 (and over a weekend), the information to the market reversed: European central banks announced a surprise five-year moratorium on all new sales of gold held in official reserves, further saying that they would also limit the amount of their gold lending. This was a massive information shock to the market—a double-whammy: (1) a selling moratorium from the largest holders of gold; and (2) limits on gold lending.

Against this background, we have to also remember that significant gold forward selling was an entrenched hedging strategy of the industry after almost two decades of declining prices. After all, selling gold short and forward was the no-brainer trade of the 1980s and 1990s. The longer it went on, the shorter the market became. But suddenly there was completely new—and after 20 years of declining value—almost incomprehensible information in the market and it spelled a possible paradigm shift on the horizon. The market was caught utterly short and with its pants down. It panicked at the prospect of having to scramble for gold to cover the forward selling and contracted lending needs.

Looking at Figure 3.16, we see the first pattern feature of the *knock on the door*. (In this example, an extended price trend lasting over two decades was violated in a matter of days.) This move may have seemed insignificant in the months following the announcements as the market settled down and appeared to remain in a downtrend, but the knock foreshadowed and announced to us what was to come.

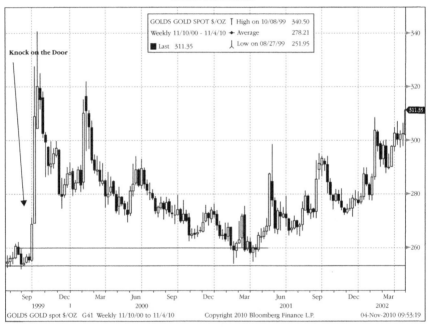

Knock on the Door

FIGURE 3.16 Gold Spot $/oz
Source: Copyright 2010 Bloomberg Finance LP.

Figure 3.16 also shows that after this knock on the door the market continued to drift in its downward direction over the next months, but never to exceed the cyclical lows of the Gold spot market. Relative to the duration of the almost-20-year downtrend, this was a very short amount of time. In spite of what was an actual pounding on the door at the time, trends of this duration and magnitude do not completely turn around in a day or a week. But something had changed.

Following the knock, the dynamics and behavior of the downward trend had taken on a different characteristic. Momentum was reduced and the degree of price descent was shallower. The dominant tribe driving the selling was getting weak and breaking away from the herd. This is not too different from the police arriving at a party in the late hours. Once they have come and gone, the party is no longer the same; it's time to go home. This price pattern after the knock on the door in Figure 3.16 indicates that new sentiment was entering the market and telling us of the market shift.

Consider this same pattern in a single equity and in a shorter time scale: Schlumberger Ltd. (SLB) had been in a downward trend throughout 2007 and 2008. Unlike the highly unusual "V" reversal pattern seen by many equities in spring 2008, SLB displayed a more definitive and classic reversal pattern than most equities, announcing the late 2009 spring rally. SLB kicked off with a knock on the door in the first days of January 2009 when prices broke the 2008 trend-line, albeit stopping and rejecting price at a resistance cluster (a gap in this case). See Figure 3.17.

FIGURE 3.17 Schlumberger Ltd. with a Knock on the Door
Source: Copyright 2010 Bloomberg Finance LP.

Following this move, SLB sold off through January, to test the lower range of the support and to make multiple probes on low momentum with and within a narrow price range (as we saw in Figure 3.9). By March 2009, SLB had broken out of a multi-month trend, moving up almost 30 percent from its lows of 37.07 in December 2008 and doubling in price by March 2010. See Figure 3.18. Note that the previous resistance around 55.00 is now the new support range.

FIGURE 3.18 Schlumberger Ltd., Price Progression after the Knock on the Door
Source: Copyright 2010 Bloomberg Finance LP.

Here, as in the example of the Gold market, the knock-on-the-door price pattern gave us important information announcing the potential of an imminent directional move up—a trend shift, a change of power and dominance driving price and weakening the previously dominant selling tribe. Observing the features of this price action, we see four things:

1. A trend-line break after an accelerated and sustained move down—yearly, weekly, daily, or intraday, depending on your trading time frame
2. Loss of price momentum after the first knock that broke the trend (which can be measured with standard momentum indicators if you want to verify what you see)
3. Probing within the borders of support and resistance
4. A possible test move below support and resistance to be met with immediate buying and rejection of lower prices

Some traders will recognize a *rounding bottom* in this example. It shows the characteristics and details of this complete pattern constellation. As this pattern unfolded, after the first knock on the door of the pattern, SLB should have been on our radar as a likely real deal.

The knock on the door announces a shift in the market. It is characterized by a trend break and a change in momentum following the trend break. Let's look at this pattern in daily action on the most liquid grain market—CBOT Corn—and the same or similar knock on the door appearing in both a daily and an intraday 30-minute chart of the front month Corn contract. See Figures 3.19 and 3.20.

FIGURE 3.19 CBOT Front Month Corn, Daily
Source: Copyright 2010 Bloomberg Finance LP.

Before we leave this pattern, take a closer look at a feature that often appears to (apologies in advance for the pun) bite us. The knock is not a pattern in isolation. Just as it *precedes* a significant market move on the horizon, it is accompanied and *followed by* a recognizable pattern that we'll call the *snake*.

The Snake

All of the definitive reversal moves seen in the previous figures were preceded by something else: a market caught in a narrow range—boundaries of price oscillating between a very narrow range of support and resistance. (Again, S&R is the keystone of all price patterns.) This is

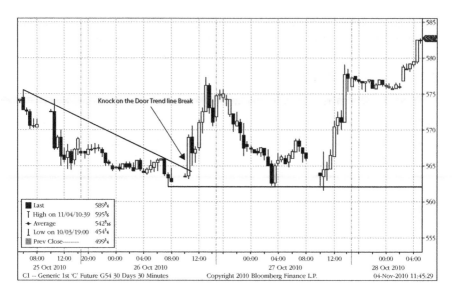

FIGURE 3.20 CBOT Front Month Corn, 30-minute Chart
Source: Copyright 2010 Bloomberg Finance LP.

our snake-in-the-grass (sometimes referred to as the *phase of the snake*). We will see it appear again as a feature of a broader pattern constellation.

A snake sits sunning itself, going nowhere other than looking for food, shelter, or a mate. It progresses forward with a winding, laterally undulating movement in which the body segments are oriented in one direction, pushing forward in contact with the ground, while the other segments are lifted up. This makes for its peculiar, yet highly coordinated, rolling motion. As a snake moves along, leaving a track of wavy or straight lines in the sand, it is silent and slow and attracts little attention. And such are the markets characterized by the snake.

A market at this time is slow and boring for the trader and attracts little attention. Traders want action, excitement, and noise. We see and hear nothing, and tend to go looking for action elsewhere. The important message of silence is ignored. But as with a real-life snake-in-the-grass that we do not see or hear, a quiet market in the phase of the snake is also dangerous. A snake needs to eat and will strike its prey.

What are the characteristics of the snake? The snake undulates within the price range of support and resistance, often with the market noise (in this instance, perhaps with the hissing of pressure?). Many walk away from a market that is messy and noisy with nothing really going on—creeping along, or on a seemingly straight line over time. Directional moves to the up- or downside are too small to practically trade. Low-risk entry and exit

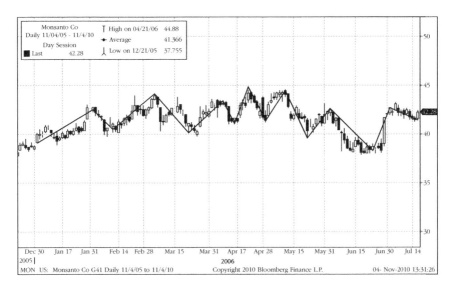

FIGURE 3.21 Monsanto Co., Daily. in the Phase of the Snake
Source: Copyright 2010 Bloomberg Finance LP.

are difficult. In spite of this these markets, too, should demand our attention. See Figure 3.21.

The Ambush

As mentioned, the snake needs to eat. To do this, it sometimes makes a move counter to its direction as it winds up to strike its prey. This is the *ambush* or *coil* of the snake and is illustrated in Figure 3.22.

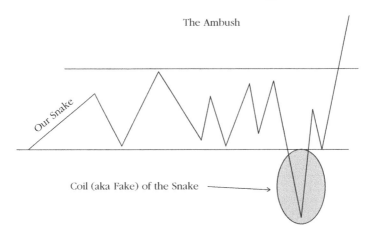

FIGURE 3.22 Ambush Characterized by Extreme Short-Term Price Swing

For commodity traders, the dynamics behind the ambush might be blamed on "fishing for stops." The futures market exists to facilitate price discovery. That is its economic purpose and it is the work of the speculator and short-term trader. We cannot fight the "ambushers," per se (those fishing for stops and participating in the collective market price-discovery mechanism), so instead of worrying about the possibility of the specialist or market-maker going for your stops, look out for the information revealed by their handiwork and recognize it. When you do, it will tell you about the true nature of the market and what might come. Regardless of the triggers for a move like this, the action around the ambush sends us a message.

SPOTTING THE AMBUSH   A heavily traded equity as I write is Apple Inc. (AAPL), trading around $260.00. At the end of 2002, a directional shift for Apple was foreshadowed with the knock. As in previous examples, there were characteristic signs of what emerged as the real deal. With the knock, the price of Apple broke to the upside, violating the long-term accelerated downward spiral in prices. Following the knock pattern (as often is the case, and as we saw in the examples of Gold and SLB earlier in the chapter), prices returned to the lower range of support and resistance. On reduced momentum, the price slithered like a snake between 6.60 and 7.80 for four long months. But the dynamics of the party were over. See Figure 3.23.

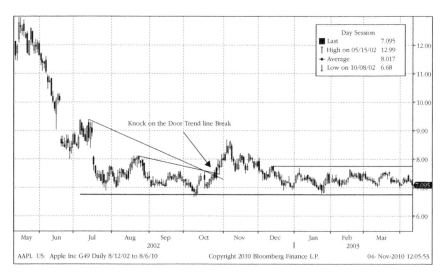

FIGURE 3.23 Apple Inc., Daily. In the Phase of the Snake After the Knock on the Door
Source: Copyright 2010 Bloomberg Finance LP.

In short, over this period of time, it looked like the market was doing nothing; but for us, AAPL was on our radar because we had spotted the three elements of the pattern constellation:

1. Foreshadowing of a knock, which characteristically broke/violated a long-term trend-line
2. Loss of previous momentum, as price returned to within the support and resistance range
3. Price entering a very narrow range over a period of many weeks' sessions—the phase of the snake.

THE COIL BEFORE THE STRIKE (A.K.A., THE FAKE)   After the knock, when price returned back within the boundaries of support and resistance, on low momentum and into a narrow range, the price then broke through long-term support. See Figure 3.24. This is the coil of price in the opposite direction of the destined price move.

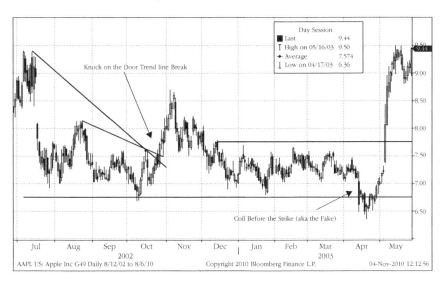

FIGURE 3.24 Price Coil Before Strike
Source: Copyright 2010 Bloomberg Finance LP.

As in every coiling move belonging to this pattern, the break is brief, proving over the next few trading sessions to be the pretender. The break was not sustained, returned to the channel break point, and then by the end of April was back within the price boundary and closing on the highs of the day. The three features of this upside shift reversal pattern are:

1. A knock on the door after a sustained trend down that violated longer-term price trends.

2. The return to defined boundaries of previous support and resistance, where the market goes into the narrow snake pattern.
3. Sometimes, just as in nature, we observe a counter windup coiling action and rapid break (or the fake) below the support boundary with an immediate a return into the boundary—price rejection of the lower range. This signals not only a false breakdown (the *pretender*) but the coiling and reverse motion before the snake strikes and surprises us all.

If we look at Figure 3.24, on May 5, the pattern that put AAPL on our radar was confirmed as price broke powerfully to the upside in a classic breakout fashion. Developing a trading strategy around identifying a knock, recognizing the appearance of a snake (with a possible coil move), and concluding with a firm rejection of price at the lower boundaries as price moves into a new range, following the preceding pattern constellation, is *not* bottom picking. It is trading the reversal on a sound, pattern-based strategy. This pattern tells us much about the behavior of the market participants and the possible emerging dominance of a new tribe.

Identifying low-risk entry points against this pattern and maintaining a forward-looking anticipation of price behavior keeps one in a trade with less risk of being shaken out of the market. If one is shaken out by the ambush price move, or needs to exit a position, it is emotionally easier to reenter the trade as you visualize the possible developing reversal pattern that kicked off with the knock on the door.

Conclusion

In this chapter, we looked at specific reversal pattern constellations to the upside. But what about a reversal to the downside—is it a mirror-reflection of a price turnaround to the upside? We read sometimes that all you have to do is turn a chart upside-down (if it were only that simple!), but is this so? The answer is *yes and no.* For some very basic textbook patterns such as *head and shoulders* or *V tops*, perhaps it is. But when we think about it, the conditions leading up to the breakdown in price are not the same. Accordingly, the dynamics and behavior of price in a reversal to the downside are unique to a market in selling mode. In Chapter 4 we will look at two large downside reversal pattern constellations.

Before we move on to the next chapter, though, look again at Figures 3.11, 3.12, 3.13, and 3.14 and tell me if you can now spot the real-deal reversals to the upside versus the pretenders.

(If you need a hint, Figures 3.11 and 3.12 are the pretenders, and Figure 3.13 is the real deal.)

CHAPTER 4

A Downside Reversal

"I found it too," replied the goatherd, "but never picked it up or even went close to it, for fear that it might bring bad luck, and that I might have to return it as stolen property—the devil's a cunning one, and things are always showing up at a man's feet to make him trip and fall when he's least expecting it."
—*The Ingenious Hidalgo Don Quixote de la Mancha* by Miguel de Cervantes Saavedra. [Translated by John Rutherford, Penguin Books, London (2003), p. 193.]

In Chapter 3, we discussed pattern and price to the upside reversal. Many times, traders ask, "Is a market shift reversal to the downside a mirror-opposite of the same patterns to go long? Is it so simple that all we need to do is turn a chart upside down to make a decision?" My answer is: If *only* it were that simple.

Market tops or topping patterns are described as *key reversals* (a new high day with a close at or near the low of the trading session) or *rounding tops, heads and shoulders,* or *three black birds*. These are lively and accurate metaphors of patterns pointing to price action that could head south. However, these colorful and descriptive top reversal patterns taken out of context, or in isolation, may often hint at only a short-term trading approach.

There are perhaps hundreds of identifiable market-shift pattern constellations. For our purposes here, this chapter concentrates on two large and complex downward reversal patterns, including the price conditions leading up to a formation pointing to a major market trend shift. As we zero in on these market tipping points, we will also consider the elements of pattern constellations and how they unfold in multiple time scales. Metaphors for two distinct and identifiable patterns of price action are *Icarus* and the *Titan*.

Icarus and the Air up There

Icarus fell to his death after his father, Daedalus, had warned him not to fly too close to the sun. Daedalus was a highly skilled craftsman and he and his son Icarus were held prisoner for years in King Minos's labyrinth prison. While languishing in prison, and with much time on his hands, the skilled Daedalus carefully crafted wings from feathers and wax for a flight to escape. He spent years preparing the wings. Meanwhile, his very young son gathered feathers and the guards of the prison assumed it was nothing more than a boy at play. By the time Icarus was just short of young manhood, and right before their flight, Daedalus warned his son that if he flew too low, the spray of the ocean would soak the feathers and make his wings too heavy. And worse, Daedalus warned, if he flew too close to the sun, the heat would rapidly melt the wax and the wings would break apart: "Icarus, my son, I charge you to keep at a moderate height, for if you fly too low the damp will clog your wings, and if too high the heat will melt them. Keep near me and you will be safe."[1]

As they made their flight to escape, Icarus became ecstatic by the thrill of moving through the air and the increasing height, ignoring his father's pleas to not fly too high. As Icarus's sense of unlimited ability and excitement grew, he soared higher and higher into the sky, completely disregarding his father's calls of caution. He flew so high the sun melted the wax, the wings immediately broke apart, and Icarus fell to his death.

The message behind the story of Icarus is not only that the recklessness of youth, when ignoring the guidance of their elders, might have ruinous consequences; it also tells us that at the height of a sense of well-being— when thrill consumes us and there seem to be no limits or hurdles in the way of possibilities—we can become careless, deaf and blind to the warnings around us as our emotion-filled perceptions control our actions. We reject words of warning and rational thought in this state and only self-satisfaction guides our actions. This Greek myth is the metaphor for how this state rapidly and inevitably ends in disaster.

Unlike most trend reversals and unfolding selloffs, the fall phase of Icarus is announced suddenly from within a single day to a few days. This usually shocks us all as the Icarus pattern, like that of the mythological tale, builds over months and years under conditions where we have come to believe in a single possibility: that the market will continue only higher. External warnings, even a sudden increase in extreme price volatility in both directions, are ignored.

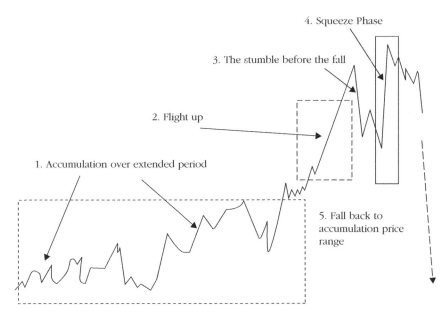

FIGURE 4.1 Conceptual Pattern of Icarus

As seen in Figure 4.1, the complete pattern constellation of Icarus is in five parts:

1. Accumulation leading up to the market squeeze or "flight." This is the longest phase.
2. Flight higher when the market goes into a phase of excitement. This is shorter relative to the accumulation phase and is usually accompanied by peaks in momentum.
3. The tipping point, often with a first stumble. This phase has high price volatility, and is where the dynamics of a squeeze appear, often where market participants *must* buy into a market for hedging or short covering needs.
4. Rapid fall to earth.
5. Fall to accumulation price range.

Like the mythological tale, the Icarus pattern results from dramatic events and market conditions and emotional sentiment on both sides of the pattern constellation. This pattern is surrounded with the most difficult trading conditions a market can throw at a trader: buying into the momentum of Icarus or selling into the fall. In fact, capturing Icarus's fall (shorting before the fall or even selling into it) often goes against almost all trading wisdom and advice, and our instincts.

The tipping point of the market-squeeze phase, part 3 of the Icarus pattern is exceptionally difficult to capture; and is, understandably, an unattractive trade for most market participants. Regardless, understanding and recognizing Icarus for what it is, and the rapid price direction it portends, is critical to understanding price action. For those who choose to try to exploit the Icarus pattern, though—with all the associated demands—it can be most rewarding. Icarus attracts what I call the *Prometheus traders*—those who try to, and sometimes do, capture fire. For others it can be a warning that we are in a market flight that could rapidly change.

The Squeeze When Icarus Appears and Where It Leads

What are the conditions for the market phase we recognize as a squeeze? What is a market price squeeze? The classic conditions are, for example, when borrowing is difficult (or impossible), as we saw in the brief gold market squeeze in late 1999 (which was a foreshadowing of a trend change and a knock-on-the-door pattern) and those who had to deliver or were short *had* to buy gold. Or, a squeeze can be when consumers are squeezed by a single supplier (and conversely when suppliers are squeezed by rising prices and cannot pass their increasing costs onto consumers). Regardless of the exact reasons, our concern is identifying the squeeze phase of the Icarus pattern.

When thinking about the pattern of a squeeze, is it sufficient to describe it (no matter the timeframe) as simply a price line going up at a steep 45-degree (or steeper) angle on a log chart? Or is it the breakout of a price range of support and resistance often detected by short-term trading methods? In fact, when considering single equities, many strategies target identifying candidates ripe for squeezes onto price. This is because the idea of capturing this price action is attractive as the gains are rapid on the back of sometimes-explosive moves to the upside (where, as we know, human nature is attracted to rising prices), and the logic of the trade is well understood. Short interest data is readily available and it can be plotted against price. (As an aside, there is an entire industry that concerns itself only with the short interest and the possible value of using this information for indicators.)

Our consideration is the squeeze of a market entering the Icarus pattern when market participants *must* cover their short positions. The cost to hold is now too great; it is, for example, when hedgers perceive they have to buy to secure future delivery obligations. It is when a fund manager must have the position in his or her portfolio by mandate (or even for job security). It is when momentum players—those employing strategies to buy only instruments entering new highs, for example—pour into the market. An Icarus squeeze is also supported when a market is fueled by buyers jumping on board because they are afraid of missing out on more gains and more excitement (i.e., by emotionally driven trading). A squeeze is fed by survival needs, momentum rules, and emotional fears of missing out. These conditions come together to drive price and create an imbalance. It leaves a trail of destruction as the market accommodates buying needs, attracting an ever-higher degree of speculative interest, and comes to the point where all the tribes and motivations merge together in lockstep action to the upside—inevitably leading to a deadly fall.

Market lore is filled with colorful anecdotes of the past market squeezes in our lifetime, especially those in the physical commodity markets. There will be more, and, perhaps in our rapidly developing global markets, the occurrences will become ever-more frequent. Examining past and even recent-past squeezes will help us understand how these phases were indeed setups for trades to be taken—to close out longs or enter short. Important to remember is that a squeeze of the Icarus pattern is not a breakout or merely simple short covering. It is a relentless explosion of price to the upside underpinned by the forces described above.

Market squeezes share common characteristics of behavior and events, and display very similar and identifiable price patterns. The price dynamic is not that of price on the long and healthy trend, where the market is on the road to price discovery among competing interests as the herds move without dissonance. It is the violent and out-of-control rampage of price, where price reaches highs we thought unimaginable just a few short months or weeks ago. It is a time in the market when fear and excitement are in competition for the passions of participants and seemingly ever-higher prices are accepted. Figure 4.2 shows that a squeeze condition before the inevitable fall can last for months.

Icarus is often seen during the last phases of a long-term secular bull, as in the most recent bull phase of the energy market reflected in the price chart of Crude Oil futures in Figure 4.2. Not all markets end with an Icarus pattern, but as in all bull markets, the early phases are supported by healthy fundamentals and associated price action, periods when the markets do not attract much attention (like young Icarus, they are still gathering their feathers for the flight).

Figures 4.2 and 4.3 show typical minor bull and bear cycle retracements (or corrections of 10 to 30 percent to the downside) and we can see that, relative to the length of the underlying bull market leading up to the squeeze, the Icarus phase is short. These examples show how markets start in a healthy directional upward trend over a price cycle of months or even years. This action can have a stealth feature as it starts. Remember, like the prison guards watching over Daedalus and Icarus, no one really pays too much attention to the phase of gathering feathers. These are slow incremental waves up, little noticed by the broader market and with hardly any notice from the external market and general public. Setbacks of 5 to even 30

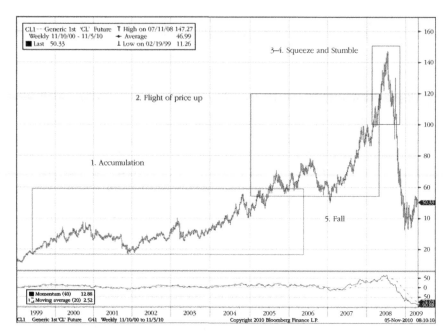

FIGURE 4.2 Icarus, Crude Oil, First Month Futures
Source: Copyright 2010 Bloomberg Finance LP.

percent are often seen along the way, but in the later stages of this secular market cycle, price accelerates on relative extremes of momentum, as seen in the previous charts.

As experienced squeeze traders (those who buy into the momentum of short covering, for example) will warn us, the duration of a squeeze phase is short, and the end of the squeeze can happen almost in an instant. While much of the industry strives to capitalize on the squeeze, we want to identify patterns of price action leading up to and during the squeeze phase, and finally the pattern triggers for the possible end of the squeeze. See Figure 4.4. Note here that the market experienced healthy pullbacks of 20 percent or more, each taking a few weeks. The tipping point for wheat was not only when momentum was at extreme levels in February and March 2008, but when we had a retracement down (extreme price rejection) of over 20 percent in just a few short days in the last week of February 2008. The market was stumbling.

Good judgment says never stand in front of a charging herd, or the mob. If you care about your well-being, do not try to reason with a mob on the run. At the same time, we know that at some point, the mob will exhaust itself and break apart. It always does. But when and how?

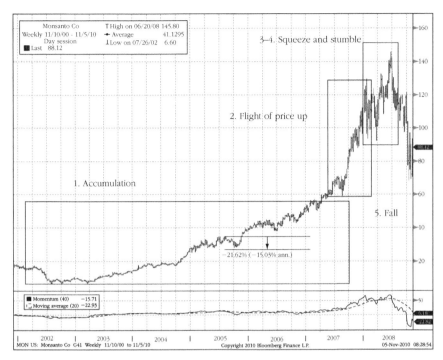

FIGURE 4.3 Ongoing Icarus in Monsanto Corp. Weekly
Source: Copyright 2010 Bloomberg Finance LP.

It can happen suddenly, or start slowly, where only the most observant detect the signs of a market about to tire, break apart, and suddenly or gradually change direction as new forces play into the marketplace. (Think back to Figure 2.4 in Chapter 2 depicting breakup.) Attempting to capture the point and then taking a position against the still-apparent and dominant stampeding herd thundering in the other direction is an undertaking only for the most disciplined strategy. It is a move for traders with a clear understanding of why the trade is taken and what the market is capable of, a trader with complete, solid self-management, including a plan of action for all eventualities. It is not for everyone. Yet, regardless of our trading style and methods, it behooves us all to understand the dynamics of the unfolding Icarus pattern.

We've all heard stories of traders calling it just right but not making the trade—the *woulda-shoulda-coulda* trades, the big ones that got away. For instance, an experienced broker named Rob Mastros of Tradeport Inc. recently told me about a client who was building up a significant short position in Crude while it was in Icarus during 2008. "Unfortunately," Rob said, "he called the top by about 35 cents, but we had to blow out the guy in oil. He had *way* too many positions on, so management of the clearing

FIGURE 4.4 CBOT Wheat, Weekly. Identify all phases of Icarus.
Source: Copyright 2010 Bloomberg Finance LP.

FCM [Futures Commission Merchant] closed his entire position. We couldn't do anything about it. The FCM was afraid he could not send the margin in time. And they would be stuck with his massive loss." To further clarify, Rob went on, "the client had previous positions (shorts) from a few dollars lower, so it kinda looked like he was really going for it in a big way. With every dollar higher this guy sold even more. But the markets didn't blow him out, the FCM did. He might have been able to hold onto the position," Rob continued, "or the market might have thrown him out first. Every tick against him was a huge paper loss near the end before he was finally taken out. If he were able to keep the position, he probably never would have needed to work again. We'll never know. . . ."

Rob's story shows an example of a trader leveraging up, who may or may not have been good for the margin while putting his brokerage at enormous risk and ignoring the rules of the game. In this situation, be warned that your broker can pull the plug at any time, and if your partners and brokers in the game sense danger to themselves, they will.

Why tell this story? When considering the Icarus pattern, it is not about picking tops but recognizing the conditions of a top. If we can do that with care and attention, a disciplined and possibly highly rewarding trading strategy can be applied. Being "right" and perfect timing are not important for ultimate success. Rob's trader, gunning for the big hit, was fighting the market to be right at some point. The trader lost a bundle, forgetting, perhaps, that his position put his FCM in a position where he *could have* cost them many hundreds of thousands of dollars. Perhaps the monkeys Hope and Greed were pulling the levers. What broker wants to go home with that on his book and worry about his own liability in the morning? Neither the market, nor the brokers, nor the market-makers cared about this trader's position.

I have got off the subject of patterns. But this story still leads into the question: How do we know when the thundering herd will tire, stumble, and fall? What is its tipping point, and how can we recognize and rationally attempt to capitalize on it?

Recognize the Tipping Point

The price action of the squeeze behind Icarus is not random. It is driven by human needs and emotion, not a series of random events or healthy competing interests and motivations in the market as in the accumulation phase. Nearing the final and flight phase of Icarus, the market is in a squeeze and moves in the lockstep as described in Chapter 2. It takes on the irrational characteristics of humanity and not the rationality of coherent markets, pricing utility, or actual demand and supply. And like many unpleasant things in life, we may not need a definition, because we know it when we see it (see Figures 4.5 and 4.6).

Let's look more closely at these recent Icarus patterns. But first, when analyzing the squeeze phase of Icarus we are going to move outside of price action alone and touch on indicators derived from price.

MOMENTUM We have covered the caveat that indicators help us quantify price yet run the danger of removing us from the price action itself. With the heavy use of indicators, we risk trading the indicator and not the price and market. So without losing the meaning of price action behind an indicator, we will use momentum here to help us capture one of the most difficult trades. Without resorting to elaborate measurements of rate of change or momentum, we will use a simple 40-period momentum reading and plot a simple 20–50-period moving average of the momentum rate.

The Momentum indicator measures and shows the rate of change in price. Values above zero indicate price is going up, and below zero price is going down. Of course, we see this without an indicator telling us. (Using the numerical reading is highly valuable when scanning many, even hundreds, of instruments.) Our interest is not in using an oscillator to measure

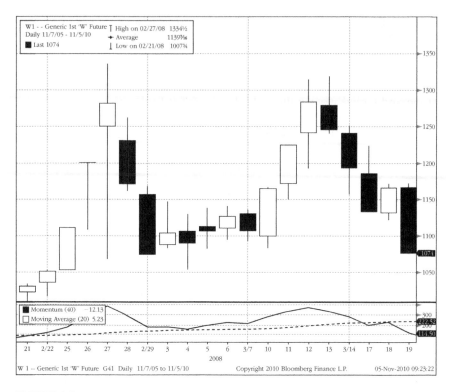

FIGURE 4.5 CBOT Wheat, Daily, during the Squeeze and Stumble Days of Icarus
Source: Copyright 2010 Bloomberg Finance LP.

whether a market is going up or down, but to quantify and capture the extremes of rate of change like the ones seen in the Icarus constellation. Momentum is simply calculated as the ratio of today's price relative to the price several (N) periods ago:

$$MOMENTUM = CLOSE(i)/CLOSE(i–N)*100$$

where

CLOSE(i) = the closing or average price of the current bar
CLOSE(i–N) = the closing or average bar price N periods ago

Using a 40-period with a 20–50-period moving average of the momentum may sound too extensive, because general traders and packaged applications use short-term momentum readings, but we are considering the longer-term price action and absolute extremes of price action around the Icarus pattern. So using a longer period would apply. These periods smooth the oscillator and give, I believe, a more careful reading of the price action against the momentum indicators. For Icarus, our intent is not to use

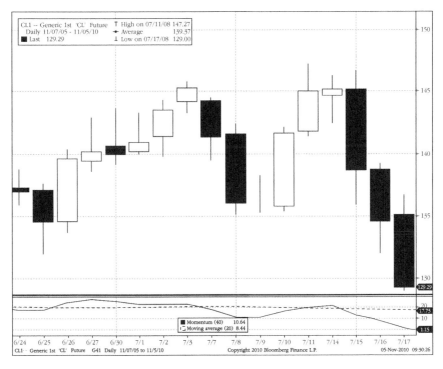

FIGURE 4.6 Crude Oil Futures, Daily, during the Squeeze and Stumble Days of Icarus
Source: Copyright 2010 Bloomberg Finance LP.

the momentum readings to *go with* momentum but rather to *fade* momentum. We are trying to identify and capture a market out of balance, which is opportunity. Let's look at the recent squeeze of Crude Oil from 2007 to 2008 as shown in Figure 4.7.

The uptrend of this market kicked off in 2001 and early 2002. (Revisit the charts—both daily and weekly—of that trend shift in Chapter 3.) In 2008, the last phase of the bull market went into squeeze phase, alerting us to the possibilities of an unfolding Icarus pattern. As seen in Figure 4.7, it is characterized by a steady increase in weekly price momentum relative to price over the past five years or more. So far, this is still an indication of a strongly uptrending market with increasing but healthy momentum.

As we enter into the second quarter of 2008, however, we can see an extreme reading of momentum against strongly rising prices. We know the condition cannot sustain itself any more than any object moving at extreme speed can continue at such extreme velocity. At some point it will seek equilibrium. Yet by all measures, including the background sentiment at the time, the squeeze is on and the phase of Icarus has kicked in. Characteristic is that price corrections are short and shallow during the price flight. (See Figure 4.8.)

FIGURE 4.7 Crude Oil Squeeze
Source: Copyright 2010 Bloomberg Finance LP.

With the increase in momentum was also the typical rise in volatility to the upside with the characteristic series of false reversals, which prove to brief setbacks in price masquerading as daily reversals (again a pattern in isolation). These are moves that shake the shorter-term traders out of the market, introducing covering by new short interest, and are anathema (as I well know) for swing traders. Other than the simple and classical reversal, what distinguishes the short setback reversal from the real deal? Of course, we never know with certainty until after the fact, but when considering the Crude Oil chart in Figure 4.9, we see a few guidelines.

Look carefully at the selloff in 2006 shown in the weekly chart in Figure 4.9. It initially met the characteristic of a trend shift or change and in fact proved to be an excellent shorting opportunity. The daily price action during this period gave strong alerts, showing a new high with price rejection as resistance over multiple trading sessions and a breakdown through daily support ranges, as seen in Figure 4.10 on page 75. (We will see that these very S&R ranges determine price pattern structure in the future.) But as we see, this market condition was a healthy correction. Nor were momentum or volatility at extremes. And the correction downward unfolded over weeks, not days or a day. This was not an Icarus fall.

FIGURE 4.8 Crude Oil, Weekly, in the Flight up with Shallow Corrections
Source: Copyright 2010 Bloomberg Finance LP.

Indeed, there was a three-month selloff against the primary trend and price support, one with a strong weekly reversal to the upside in mid-December. For traders into the short side of this pattern, however, one sees repeated warnings that the upward trend remains intact into the early fall of 2006.

Then, as you can see in Figure 4.9, in late 2006, there was a trend break to the downside. By all measures, the bull market of 2001–2006 was over. In the first weeks of 2007, there was a break through major support around 55.00 as defined over the previous bull market (it was a previous resistance level, as can be seen in Figure 4.2).

The warning of strength in the market was that this selloff at a key price range met immediate price rejection of lower prices and a return back into previous support. Then, we see this support holds with each additional test downward over the next few weeks. By September 2007, we had not only recovered completely, but exceeded the highs of 2006. This confirmed that we were, indeed, still in the long-term secular bull market that started in 2001.

FIGURE 4.9 Crude Oil Futures, Weekly, July 2006–August 2007
Source: Copyright 2010 Bloomberg Finance LP.

The price action between November 2006 and into the spring of 2007 is part of a pattern we will call *the Valley of the Kings,* which is common to secular bull markets; we will go into it in more detail in Chapter 6.

The price dynamic described above is more often seen in the commodity markets and less so in the general equity markets. The *stumble* phase before the fall often takes longer to unfold, as we see in Figure 4.3 of Monsanto Corp. So, next, let's look at the two examples of a classical Icarus pattern as seen in the equity markets presented in Figures 4.11 and 4.12 on pages 76 and 77.

Note that during the flight up corrections are brief and minor. The stumble phase before the fall has increased volatility in both directions and extends over many weeks. After liquidation throughout 2002 and 2001, CSCO bottomed out at 8.12 in October 2002.

Readers will note in Figure 4.12, the chart for Goldman Sachs Group, that price pullbacks were minor in the flight phase and that momentum met an extreme as price volatility in both directions kicked in.

FIGURE 4.10 Crude Oil Futures, Daily, April 2006–October 2006
Source: Copyright 2010 Bloomberg Finance LP.

Summary

The final phase of the Icarus pattern includes:

1. An accelerated price progression to the upside relative to the entire period considered.
2. An extreme reading in price momentum. To smooth this out, adjust the measurement to a longer time period of, for example, 40. We do this because short-term momentum readings are capturing only that—the very short-term (which is not relevant to capturing the price action of markets in the extreme stages of longer-term trend extension buildup). The preceding figures show an overlay of a 50-period exponential moving average onto the momentum. This aids in quantifying a divergence of the price action and momentum. As seen in Figure 4.12, for example, the moving average (MA) crossover of momentum, which has been discovered from price, can be a trade signal.

FIGURE 4.11 Cisco Systems Inc. in Icarus between October 1999 and October 2000
Source: Copyright 2010 Bloomberg Finance LP.

3. Against the conditions above, an observation of a series of daily or intra-day reversal patterns to the downside where price is repeatedly rejected at Resistance over the time period considered. (See Figures 4.9 and 4.10.)

Sometimes the above conditions will come together and we then add a price point from a previous and long-term resistance range. This may be more applicable in commodity markets because they are markets for cyclical and renewable resources. Equity markets are capital markets reflecting overall capital growth, so the multiyear price data and identification of previous price rejection from years back has, in my opinion, less bearing on technical price action considerations. See Figure 4.13 on page 78.

When possible, in detecting Icarus we can also consider sentiment and refer to put/call ratios, or measuring short interest in equities (all examples of how traders attempt to measure and quantify sentiment). The patterns of price tell us about sentiment and these indicators with price patterns may complete the picture. With advances emerging in information technology, methods to map and measure news coverage around a topic, commodity,

FIGURE 4.12 Goldman Sachs Group Inc. in Icarus Flight-and-Tumble Phase Starting August 2007 and into March 2008
Source: Copyright 2010 Bloomberg Finance LP.

or equity, capturing clusters of news against price, may also give us insights into sentiment extremes.

There is another thing to think about. When analyzing markets that appear to be in extremes, we can ask ourselves whether financial broadcasts or the general financial press are bullish when the price action we are seeing does not match up to the rhetoric. Is there ecstasy in the public arena while we see evidence of ongoing price rejection in the market?

Our next downside reversal pattern is less dramatic in the final buildup and crash to earth but can be much more dramatic in the actual consequences and significance.

The Titan Constellation

This pattern's name comes from another apt mythological allegory. The Titans were the sons and daughters of Uranus and Gaea (Heaven and Earth).

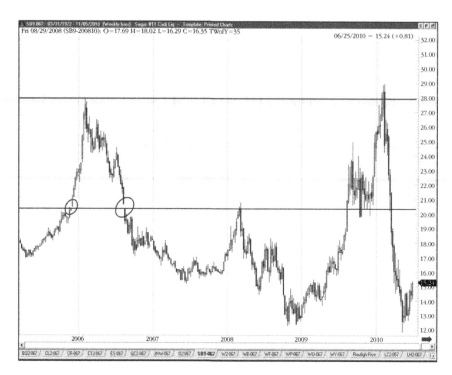

FIGURE 4.13 World Sugar No. 11 Front Month Future in Icarus
Source: Genesis Financial Technologies, Inc.

After killing off their father Uranus, the Titans ruled the world. Oceanus, Rhea, Atlas, and others comprised the Titans. Everything came together under them and it was considered a long Golden Age. After a long time and by great forces of godly nature they were overthrown by the Olympians, who then gained supremacy in the world of the gods. After this defeat under the Olympians, Zeus, and his siblings, the Titans, were never to rule again.

The second reversal pattern presented here reflects market weight and is referred to as the *Titan* pattern constellation because it is a reversal that happens slowly and gradually, leaving most traders unaware of the slow erosion of the market and the powerful, often unrecognized, forces undermining it. Ironically, and just as in the case of the tragically aptly named ship, *Titanic*, few market participants see the "iceberg" on the horizon and those that do are ignored or the meaning of their warnings is not understood.

The Titan market pattern, the final stages of the selling off are rapid. The most recent titanic constellation experienced in the markets was in financial stocks. Look at Figure 4.14, Colonial Bank (CNB). Can you see why this equity's action is a titan pattern?

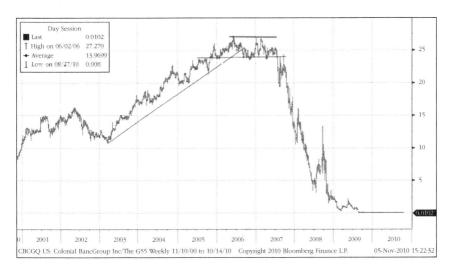

FIGURE 4.14 The Colonial Bank Group Inc., Weekly, 2001–2010
Source: Copyright 2010 Bloomberg Finance LP.

Colonial Bancgroup was one of the largest regional banks in the United States and traded on the New York Stock Exchange and now is traded in the tattered realms of the pink sheets (an over-the-counter market for stocks that are extremely thinly traded, closely held, or, as in the case of CNB, in bankruptcy). It is a slain equity, a former god. "In the bottom of this pit, the Titan race, which warred against the gods, lie prostrate. . . ."[2]

Colonial Bancgroup flourished in the boom of the late 1990s and early 2000s, especially in the state of Florida. At its height it had over $25 billion in assets and 346 branches or outlets across five states. Like Washington Mutual, it was a Titan of the U.S. banking and mortgage industry but in 2009 it was rapidly shut down by the Federal Deposit Insurance Corporation (FDIC).[3]

After buying 25 banks in Florida between 1996 and 2007, it was a big player in real estate loans and became a "mortgage warehouse," providing short-term loans to third-party mortgage brokers. It is said that its mortgage lending in Florida alone left the bank with $1.7 billion in nonperforming loans.[4] As I write, *The Washington Post* is reporting on the consequences of a civil lawsuit launched by the Securities and Exchange Commission against Taylor Bean, a mortgage brokerage firm. It says, "The Company would borrow money from Colonial to buy FHA-insured home loans from small lenders. It would pool the loans into securities and sell them to investors."[5]

These sordid financial details are an example of schemes that contributed to the crash of the U.S. housing market and related banking services between 2007 and 2009. As with any disaster of that magnitude, the details

FIGURE 4.15 CNB 2002-2006, Weekly
Source: Copyright 2010 Bloomberg Finance LP.

and understanding of the events leading up to the breakdown or failure
may take years to fully identify and understand. We'll leave that to economists, regulators, and financial historians, and for our purposes, look at the
important messages communicated to us by the price patterns of Colonial
Bancgroup from 2002 through 2006 (see Figure 4.15).

Unlike patterns we've seen in the figures on Icarus, here we have a
healthy upward growth of CNB from early 2002 through 2006. (In fact,
you may notice that the bottoming shift-reversal pattern in 2002–2003 is
the reversal-upward pattern constellation, including the knock on the door
and the coil, described in Chapter 3.) The market for CNB continued on
its upward climb in textbook fashion showing minor trend channels with
higher highs and lower lows. Previous resistance morphed into new support. As we see in Figure 4.15, life was good and every pause or setback
was an opportunity to buy. But then CNB went into the extended trading
range, from late 2005 and into summer 2007: The S&R range was much
more extensive in range and time relative to the previous three years. Price
dynamic had changed.

As we take a closer look at Figure 4.16, we start to see possibly the first
technical crack in CNB in summer of 2007. (There was a shift. The herd was
momentarily spooked with members making a quick exit.) The first trend-line
break in July was the foreshadowing of a larger move on the horizon. The
large cycle may not yet be over, but there is a warning: Something may be
on the horizon and the price action is firing signal, a foreshadowing.

I remember before the initial price break there were discussions about
the level of loans to reserves for CNB. Concerns about the concentration

FIGURE 4.16 Move that Unfolded over Almost 18 Months, CNB, Weekly, 2005–2007
Source: Copyright 2010 Bloomberg Finance LP.

of loans to a single regional market (Florida) were also privately voiced by analysts and on anonymous discussion boards. Then, in the summer of 2007 (just as the market hit the iceberg) the CEO publicly complained the public was down on Florida for no reason. He said, "Everybody thinks Florida is going to fall into the Gulf of Mexico. Trust me, Florida is still a great place to be."[6] Considering the honesty of the actual price action of the time, the market price action gave us a clear warning. But this was mostly ignored. (Think back on "What Distorts Perception" in Chapter 1.) As reported in the *New York Times* Business section in the summer of 2007, just weeks before threats of a complete banking meltdown:

> *In the stock market, banks with such concentrations have done a little worse than other banks this year. Short-interest on those stocks is up sharply, a sign that hedge funds think banks will end up owning a lot of vacant real estate, having to pay taxes on land that brings in no income. Mr. Jamison, the Las Vegas banker, scoffs at such a forecast. "It would," he told me, "be almost a perfect storm to have a meltdown in the real estate market."[7]*

The Fall of a Titan

We can zero in on the granular and daily price action of CNB leading up to the first warning when underlying price action signaled troubled waters. See Figure 4.17.

FIGURE 4.17 Daily Action of CNB between 2006 and 2007
Source: Copyright 2010 Bloomberg Finance LP.

You should note that we are still plotting momentum because it is an oscillator against the unfolding price in markets that display healthy upward trending over a long period of time. Under the Titan pattern, unlike Icarus, we are considering the divergence of momentum from price. While momentum is not at extremes in Figure 4.17, we do have momentum *diverging* from price: new price or equal highs (with rapid price rejection from new resistance) against sinking momentum. Indicators as such may be an additional filter to confirm what we already see.

Another Industry, Another Time

Another Titan from a different industry (and for many readers, a vastly different time) is American Telephone and Telegraph (ATT). In many ways the fall of AT&T was similar to the recent and still-ongoing fall for members of the now-changing banking industry. The shift in AT&T was an announcement of a new economic era and a set of new rulers arriving on the scene. The price action and associated patterns marked a change that unfolded over almost three years before finally sinking.

Figure 4.18 shows that in January 2000, on aggressive selling, AT&T broke through trend-line support from the lows of 1997, selling off to 36.00, almost 24 dollars from its peak of 60.00 per share in 1998—more than a 40 percent decline from its highs—a significant break, indeed.

FIGURE 4.18 AT&T Inc., Daily, First Warnings. December 1996–November 2001
Source: Copyright 2010 Bloomberg Finance LP.

AT&T is a large-capitalization equity with services that are key to infra-structure and the economy. It has a current market capitalization of over $150 billion and in late 2000 it was $250 billion at its peak of price. More than half of the holders of its shares are institutions.

In Figure 4.18, we see again the emerging Titan pattern with three defining characteristics:

1. Repeated price rejection between 58 and 60 over a period of two years.
2. Following this observation of price rejection over a now-longer-term resistance zone, we note a first break of the long-term trend in January 2000, when price broke down below 45.00. This, in combination with the repeated price rejection, tells us a potential battle is in the works (the very same pattern we observed in CNB in Figures 4.16 and 4.17). As in any long-term price pattern, a technical break of this nature must be taken seriously. Yet in keeping with the characteristics of the Titan pattern, we generally have time to position ourselves and take action after the first break in price as the market generally probes the highs.
3. As seen in Figure 4.18, in the fall of 2000 we see a recovery again to around 58.00 per share. Yet here—and zeroing in on the short-term action as seen in Figure 4.19—we see now, and for *the third time*, that price is continually rejected in a range over a period of weeks and *in the same price zone* as rejected earlier over the past months. Again, also note the divergence of momentum and price in November 2000.

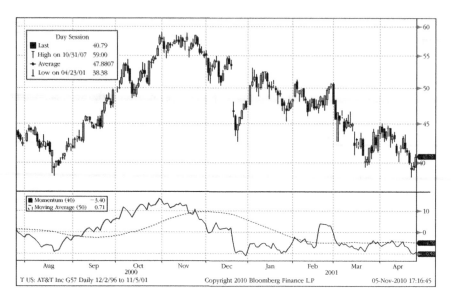

FIGURE 4.19 AT&T Inc. Repeated Rejection of Higher Prices, August 2000–April 2001
Source: Copyright 2010 Bloomberg Finance LP.

On October 26, 2001, AT&T opened gap down and over the next days slowly sold off, quietly closing the week below multiyear price support. Then over the next weeks and months, AT&T more rapidly sold off in completion of the Titan pattern constellation as seen in Figure 4.20.

What about in Commodity Markets?

In the physical commodity markets, we can expect Icarus to appear more often than the Titan pattern. And for a logical reason: Commodities are renewable resources, or, as with metals and energy, subject to cyclical forces. These markets experience disruptions in delivery, supply, and production, often coupled with shorter-term cyclical demand. A Titan pattern in commodity markets unfolds over a shorter, compressed period of time. Figures 4.21 and 4.22 provide examples.

Since October 2009, the Cocoa market has demonstrated a classic battle of the Titans. The Titan pattern has more elements than simply a "double or triple top." We see a long-term trend up with retreats to support and price acceptance within a well-defined trend channel up. As the market trends, momentum average increases along with price and then diverges from price. Unlike Icarus, the Titan top is not shot from the sky on excess and high momentum extremes but price action that gradually weakens and loses the final one of *many battles* and then retreats to the bottom of the pit "to lie prostrate."

FIGURE 4.20 Following the Titan Pattern, AT&T Inc., 1997–2005
Source: Copyright 2010 Bloomberg Finance LP.

FIGURE 4.21 Definitive Titan Fall between December 2009 and January 2010.
Cocoa Front Month Future. Daily, March 2009–November 2010
Source: Copyright 2010 Bloomberg Finance LP.

FIGURE 4.22 Close up of Titan Fall Pattern into 2010. Cocoa Front Month Future. Daily, October 2009–May 2010

Source: Copyright 2010 Bloomberg Finance LP.

As an important aside, we also need to take into account that, when considering long-term commodity future contracts, the "roll" must be factored in. There is no one right way to create the contract roll from the front and expiring months to the next month. My philosophy is to "roll 'em as I would trade 'em." For analysis, I roll the contract when volume liquidity of the back month (or second month) increases over the first (or currently traded) month.

To review: Figure 4.21 depicts a Titan pattern unfolding for Cocoa. You can see repeated price rejection above 3500/metric ton, the first definitive market rejection appeared in January 2009 and sold off into March. From here price tested what was previous support, just over 32,000/metric ton, with each test to previous support only to be immediately sold off.

Now please note and study the daily price pattern seen in Figure 4.22. It represents the price break of 2009.

We observe in all of these figures a great struggle around what was the previous price resistance or rejection. Over a period of three months there were repeated attempts by the market to seek price beyond the 3500/ton and each attempt was met with immediate market rejection of higher prices. The pattern that unfolded after the break signals us a low-risk shorting or selling (as commodity markets must be sold as easily as bought)

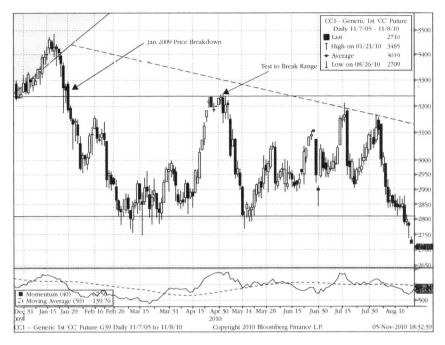

FIGURE 4.23 After the Titan Fall Pattern, Repeated Test to Resistance met With Selling. Cocoa Front Month Future. Daily, January 2009—August 2010
Source: Copyright 2010 Bloomberg Finance LP.

opportunities presented themselves, as seen in Figure 4.23. Additional low-risk selling opportunities after the initial break is characteristic of the unfolding Titan pattern constellation.

Momentum in the Trending Titan Market Pattern

Fading momentum in trending markets and an unfolding Titan pattern is not the correct application of momentum indicators to price action. More importantly, when we detect that a Titan is at battle, and unlike using momentum against an Icarus pattern, we need to consider the divergence of weekly momentum from price. In Figures 4.21 and 4.22, we see that Cocoa achieved new highs in December 2009. The momentum reading was relatively high (please note that the open interest was also at a record high, which may indicate sentiment extremes). A month later Cocoa once again tested above 3500/metric ton. This time, however, the higher price test was on falling price momentum (a key characteristic of the Titan constellation). Let's take a micro-look at the logic of trading the Titan considering momentum with the unfolding pattern.

FIGURE 4.24 Higher Price Diverging from Momentum. Cocoa Front Month Future.
Daily, October 2009–December 2010
Source: Copyright 2010 Bloomberg Finance LP.

Figure 4.24 shows a daily pattern of this market, allowing us to zero into the shorter-term price action around these critical Titan price days. In the figure, we see that on December 16, 2009, Cocoa closed at new contract highs on a solid and strong up day. The following day, though, it traded inside the range of the new-high breakout day, with no follow-through indicating indecision. For the moment, at least, new buying seems to have been exhausted. Although the market is still trending up, it has signaled a caveat. Momentum and price are diverging, as seen in Figure 4.24.

Then, as seen in Figure 4.25, on the 18th, the market showed its hand yet again by completely rejecting this price probe to new highs. We can reasonably assume that speculative short-term breakout strategies (attempting to buy into new highs) were stopped out on this strong move down where price closed at new weekly lows, and almost immediately after new contract highs! Then, a month later—true to the Titan constellation of repeated battles—prices recovered to the breakout range seen on December 16.

Over a period of three days, and at this range of December 17–18, the market firmly rejected higher prices; and with a test up again in January, the market again rejected price at this range over another three-day period. This daily action is the micro-pattern (or *fractal*, as currency traders often

FIGURE 4.25 Multiple Battles for the Titan. Cocoa Front Month Future. Daily, October 2009–February 2010
Source: Copyright 2010 Bloomberg Finance LP.

say) of the unfolding weekly pattern also observed on the larger time scale. (There are parallels of this in Elliot Wave and Gann theory, too, but that is the subject of another work.)

In this example, our Titan pattern completed with the trend channel break in late January through 3200/metric ton; and price retracement back to the break (previous support becomes new resistance) where the market sold off again. As this pattern unfolded, participants were afforded multiple opportunities for low-risk selling pattern triggers within the entire Titan pattern.

Summary

In summary, the characteristics of the Titan constellation are:

1. It unfolds over relatively long periods and with healthy trends.
2. Public participation is usually large (in equities).
3. There are multiple battles at the top range of price rejection, each affording a low-risk sell opportunity.

4. We often observe momentum and price diverging at identified resistance ranges.
5. Sentiment often diverges from unfolding price at the top ranges (bullish sentiment not confirmed by price).
6. The Titan equity generally never recovers its supremacy.

Conclusion

When looking at the downward shift patterns of Icarus and the Titan, we jumped forward and considered patterns in smaller time frames (daily) against an unfolding weekly pattern. In Chapter 5, we will take an even closer look at pattern constellations that repeat themselves in multiple time frames just as do the veins of a leaf, branches of a tree, or spiral of a shell.

The idea of price as sets of repeating order touches on topics from the mathematics of topology to even astrology, in the world of technical analysis of price, and the ideas behind theories of market structure. We will not detail these topics (Elliot Wave Theory, Price Harmonics, etc.) as there is much excellent literature already. We will examine the conceptual basis of analyzing price in multiple time frames and how this can enhance our understanding of unfolding price patterns.

CHAPTER 5

Price and Repeating Order

"It is true that most of the adventures you find don't turn out as well as what you'd like them to, because out of a hundred you come across ninety-nine usually go skew-whiff. . . . But in spite of all that, it's great to be waiting to see what's going to happen next. . . ."

—*The Ingenious Hidalgo Don Quixote de la Mancha* by Miguel de Cervantes Saavedra. [Translated by John Rutherford, Penguin Books, London (2003), p. 474.]

Expanding on the large pattern constellations considered in Chapter 4, we naturally ask: Do patterns repeat themselves? Can we see the same or similar patterns again in various time scales? Does one scale of time have anything to do with the next? Why, when we come into our office in the morning, would we look at price action in a monthly, daily, or 15-minute period to discover something we've already seen happen at a previous close? A set of daily data clearly tells us where price is, so why use various time scales to read the market when we are concerned only about what is happening now?

Throughout this chapter, we'll answer these questions and break down price and pattern to determine an overall trading strategy as a market shift unfolds.

Fractals in Price

When we talk about fractals, do we mean the ones from the growing field of fractal mathematics and geometry? Fractals from the field of mathematics gained popular interest with the computer visualization of images of fractal geometry. Or do we mean what appears as repeating patterns in objects and systems of nature, such as that of a coastline, a tree, or the individual leaves of a fern?

Considering the markets, perhaps we mean an indicator with a trading rule around increments of change or patterns that are part of a whole? Fractals are now a somewhat fashionable expression in the world of trading, technical analysis, and consideration of price patterns. It is a broadly used term with different understandings depending on the writer, the market, and one's approach to the market. But first, here is a brief layperson's background on fractals and self-similarity.

When Felix Hausdorff introduced the expression *fractal dimension* in his pioneering work on the mathematics of topology in 1918 at the University of Bonn, the Age of Fractuality in modern mathematics was launched. A set that can be assigned a fractal dimension is called a *fractal set*. The fractal dimension of the set is determined by observing optimal covering (as in topology) systems of fractal sets with decreasing diameters. In short, it was the mathematics of what is an intuitive concept of an ordering, sequencing, or arranging of the elements of any set. Approximations of fractal sets are observed in the real world: sets of surfaces and shapes of coastlines, the surface shape of a leaf, or in the "endpoints" of trees. The geometric characterizations of the simplest fractals display *self-similarity* where the shape is made of smaller copies of itself. Each copy is similar in shape to the whole, but of different sizes.

Fractals are an elegant mathematical concept that fits some structures seen in nature. Extrapolations of the mathematics of the fractal set have since been used in multiple disciplines. Consequently, the term *fractal* has taken on different meanings because its applications range from mathematics, geometry, and the physical properties such as sound waves to measuring the ocean tides in coastal engineering. After Benoit Mandelbrot made the case that markets appear to have more in common with the fractal patterns of nature than a random walk, the idea of fractals became linked to price patterns.

Many people think of fractals in the absolute sense of the mathematics of *chaos theory*.[1] While these concepts do apply to the market (which is a nonlinear, dynamic system), fractals for traders simply characterizes the idea of recurring patterns with predictive significance that can give order to what appears to be chaotic price movement.

In trading, a fractal is a repeated and similar pattern in smaller increments of time or scale. The concept of fractals in price patterns and visualization is used to try to understand infinitely complex markets as a set that organizes itself into a sort of fractal structure. Given this application of fractal geometry to price behavior, I suspect there will be a growing analysis and prediction industry created from fractals into indicators. Series of price data do exhibit characteristics of nonregular and self-similar patterns to a certain extent, so it is appealing to apply the concepts to new price-prediction models. But there may be limitations. I believe it can never be exact. The flow of price is a response to ever-changing conditions and free will, and free will always prevails over deterministic rules of fractal geometry.

Our work as traders, then, is to be in sync with the _order_ and pattern of free will and how this might organize itself into a repeating self-similar set in a marketplace driven by the behavior of its participants.

A Fractal Precedent in the History of Price and Pattern Analysis

The language to describe repetition in multiple scales also varies among and within scientific fields. And the idea of similarity of price behavior in multiple time frames precedes the more recent advances in mathematical theory and rapid computation and visual modeling.

The logic and phenomena of fractal behavior of markets were described in great detail much earlier than the 1980s by various men who did not employ the language of mathematics and physics or even use the term _fractal_. It is in fact the basis of _Elliott Wave theory_,[2] as described by R.N. Elliott in the 1930s, of repeating price patterns and cycles in various time frames. Additionally, _Gann theory_,[3] described around the same time by William D. Gann, touched on concepts behind fractal mathematics of length and time and resulting patterns. A bit earlier, Charles Dow (founder of the _Wall Street Journal_) described repeating cyclical phases of price and behavior with his presentation of the _Dow Theory_. In addition to these men, during this same time, a young mathematician in Paris, Louis Bachelier, published a thesis on pricing stock options applying the stochastics of Brownian motion to price change. (Bachelier's thesis is thought to be the first application of mathematics to finance.)

Elliott Wave theory and Gann theory were described by observant men who were not trained in mathematics or physics. Elliott was an accountant, and Gann, who had little formal education, is said to have had a strong aptitude for mathematics. At the turn of the 19th century, Gann described price behavior as adhering to observed natural laws in his work on the "Law of Vibration." In this work, price and time are broken down into repetitive squares and then projected forward. We can assume that neither he nor Elliott came across Bachelier's thesis applying the theory of Brownian motion to price movement, or stochastic heat equations to a stock-pricing model. Yet on one level, the work of these men (stochastic wave properties, repetition of motion, and organization of natural systems) was indeed related and belongs to what we now call *fractals*.

Louis Bachelier's forgotten thesis (*Théorie de la Spéculation*) has since been revised by initiatives of academics. In fact, within the past decade, "The Bachelier Finance Society" was established for "the advancement of the discipline of finance under the application of the theory of stochastic processes, statistical and mathematical theory."[4] And further,

> *Bachelier was ahead of his time and his work was not appreciated in his lifetime. In the light of the enormous importance of international derivative exchanges (where the pricing is determined by financial mathematics) the remarkable pioneering work of Bachelier can now be appreciated in its proper context and Bachelier can now be given his proper place. Bachelier's work is remarkable for herein lies the theory of Brownian Motion.[5]*

Elliott, Gann, Dow, and Bachelier, very different men and each working around the same time but unaware of each other, singularly describe in their own language (whether based on the theoretical foundation of an accountant or the brilliant and gifted mathematician) the phenomenon that price movement displays a natural structure and has a repeating order in the active markets: Dow, with a description of cyclical behavior of markets; Gann and Elliott, with an observation that markets mirrored the patterns of natural systems to be applied to predictive methods; and Bachelier, whose application of stochastic mathematics of Brownian motion could be applied to a pricing model of options on financial instruments.

Back to the Future

Elliott's observation of repeating patterns in various time frames went deeper into the nature and description of repetitive price wave cycles than the work of Dow or Gann. Rather than ideas of price acceptance and rejection (support and resistance) and with little concern for human behavior, Elliott described the market as organizing itself into a series of separate wave cycles. For example, within bull markets, there would be downward *wave corrections* against the primary bull trend. And within primary bear market cycles, there would be smaller bull market waves. Elliott described the market as organized into a three-wave cycle (consisting of a grand cycle, a super-cycle, and a primary cycle). In turn, these cycles are composed of three smaller movements that could be broken down into even smaller

units of time and price, each representative of the basic three-wave patterns. This thought process was his leap into fractals.

One view of Elliott Wave theory is that Elliott, like Gann, may have
succumbed to static application of a theory to the nonstatic market system.
Regardless, modern physics and mathematics of fractal phenomena and
geometry may bear out the ideas of R.N. Elliott, and his work might find
acceptance as a theoretical foundation of the fractals of price.

But, just as Bachelier did not have the answer to the *why* of his theory
of speculation, we also have detailed descriptions of perceived patterns but
no explanation for the apparent visual phenomena. And though Bachelier
did not have an answer for what drove markets, he did establish a rigor-
ous mathematical explanation of markets. Therefore, his work launched a
theoretical foundation of price behavior for options of future expiry. Long
after his death, Bachelier's contribution has found practical application and
is now the basis of option pricing.

Fractals in Prediction Models

Mandelbrot stated,

> *In finance, this concept is not a rootless abstraction but a theoretical
> reformulation of a down-to-earth bit of market folklore—namely, that
> movements of a stock or currency all look alike when a market chart
> is enlarged or reduced so that it fits the same time and price scale. An
> observer then cannot tell which of the data concern prices that change
> from week to week, day to day or hour to hour. This quality defines the
> charts as fractal curves and makes available many powerful tools of
> mathematical and computer analysis.[6]*

This is an alluring idea: to apply the brilliant mathematics of fractals
and rescaling to analyzing price and volatility for attempts at predictabil-
ity. It is applied in hopes of slicing current market prices into individual
moments of trading activity and then combining each separate slice to
derive a prediction of direction, duration, and target into the future. I fear
that as these methods of breaking down and analyzing larger sets of data
become ever-more elaborate there is a danger that they will become more
and more removed from the very human behavior driving the markets.

Self-Similar Fractals We See

Without going into any discussion of fractal theory and the mathematics of
fractals (the Hurst exponent[7] and Mandelbrot's work on time series data),

which is beyond not only the purpose of this book but the competencies of your author, we accept that price is determined by the market participants who are reacting not only to price information, but also to information outside of the markets and at different times. Not all participants work in the same moment nor do they make decisions based on the same kind of information or timescale of price. Operating in different time frames, we respond to events and fundamental information as time progresses; so price information in liquid active markets, therefore, must occur in multiple time frames.

Because of this, when we look at a price chart of a liquid market it is almost impossible to say what is the time scale of the data—daily, monthly, 15-minutes? My thought is that if we identify market turning points with the methods described in the previous chapters, we can then magnify the characteristic of the current prevailing price action by breaking price action down into fractals of time. A data series does not repeat itself, but the behavior of market participants does repeat regardless of time frame of participation, and it is this that creates the phenomenon of a self-similar pattern (fractal).

For example, Figure 5.1 is the complete picture of a market and price data set. This shows obvious demonstrations of cyclical behavior in waves

FIGURE 5.1 Sugar No. 11, 20 Years, Monthly
Source: Genesis Financial Technologies, Inc.

and trends over a period of 20 years. The wave patterns may also look like chaotic sound oscillations, though the pattern shown just happens to be the price of world sugar (a commodity actively traded in all parts of the world). Each bar represents a period of one month, or a one-month trading session.

Over the same period, Figure 5.2 illustrates the price of world sugar in a weekly chart. The time frame is compressed from 20 years to a week

FIGURE 5.2 Sugar No. 11, Weekly
Source: Genesis Financial Technologies, Inc.

within that time span and yet it illustrates the same price patterns and dynamics as Figure 5.1. Figure 5.3 is a daily chart of a period within this time frame, but at a different scale. We also see here similarity of price patterns. Each time frame is behaving in a similar manner to the details of the complete whole. In and of itself, this may have little application to a specific trading strategy, but the observation is important.

These figures establish the phenomenon of self-similarity of a data series presented by the price of sugar in different time periods (i.e., similarities between the 20-year monthly chart of World Sugar #11 and the 2-year daily). We can view the pattern of price progression and zoom into parts of these whole data sets and observe that the patterns are integral to the whole data sets.

FIGURE 5.3 Sugar No. 11, Daily
Source: Genesis Financial Technologies, Inc.

Fractals as More Than Prediction

Allow me to make a deliberate digression. There was a massive engineering problem to be solved in Australia in the 1950s: The famous Sydney Opera House, designed by Jorn Utzon, was still in its engineering phase, and the engineers and architects realized that the beautifully designed repeating tiled shell-like roofs could not be built as planned. The building simply would not stand without massive amounts of scaffolding and shuttering. This would, of course, result in devastation of the entire design. The engineering and design had to be completely reworked. Multiple models were built and tested, using various slopes of the shell-like roofs but one design after the other failed. Then, as one of the architects on the team was peeling an orange, his mind wandered to thinking about the form of the sphere of the orange, and he thought about the pieces of the peels he was about to toss into the trash. An epiphany moment hit. The architect may not have been thinking about the mathematics of topology or ideas of fractals in natural forms, or even stochastic waves, but a solution was found in the strength of sphere and repetition of the spherical form applied throughout the complete structure.

The successful engineering solution called for the shells of the roof to be built on the geometry of the parts of a single sphere, each an ever-smaller part of the whole yet sharing the exact same curvature of the whole (see Figure 5.4[8]).

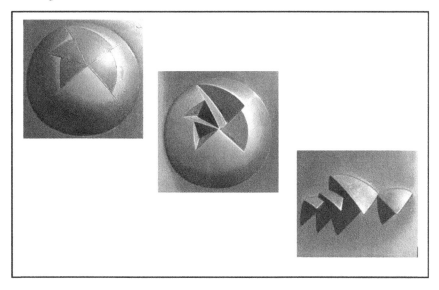

FIGURE 5.4 Sydney Opera House Facts: Jorn Utzon's Sphere
Source: www.sydneycloseup.com.

The individual shells (the roof sections) as a fraction of the whole, and with the same radius, gave the structure the static strength needed without destroying the design concept. The shell forms of the roof were subdivided into separate ribs of the circumference, and these ribs divided into ever smaller elements, down to the shape of the single roof tile. This method also allowed the parts of the shells to be cast in smaller pieces and assembled right at the construction site. The Opera House was built on a single geometrical order and repetition of shape and pattern throughout the entire structure.[9]

How simple: An outsized engineering and logistical problem was solved merely with the solutions found in the shape of a sphere and the physical forces of billions of years of organic evolution with what we now call fractals. We can similarly apply this solution to financial markets.

Fractal Repetition in Markets

If a similar structure of natural systems is found in the markets, perhaps this, too, yields strength of structure to the markets. Our challenge with visualizing a market is not to project large cycles or to develop a pricing model for options, but to seek similar order out of the apparent chaos of price action so we can act on the strength of a natural order. To do this we can break price action into shorter units of time to reveal the complete and unfolding price structure for our analysis and trade management.

We might look for convergence of pattern between and among time scales. Will the patterns repeat themselves exactly as described in fractals? No. At the very most we can observe a sort of self-similarity at some periods (as we saw in the example of sugar in the preceding figures) and, in particular, at major turning points in price cycles or market shifts.

In the real world (and we as traders are dealing with the real world, not a theoretical world) one cannot expect absolute self-similarity in the mathematical sense, but rather similarity in the behavior of price. This can be modeled and is what we look for. However, I emphasize the caveat that when observing financial markets, self-similarity should not be understood as a repetition of the exact same pattern. That is deterministic and ill-fitting for price analysis. Instead, we observe a similarity of behavior between different time scales, which are parts of the whole.

The Market Wedge and the Market Vortex

In this section, we will consider two real-world methods to analyze the same markets in multiple time scales: the *market wedge* (parts of the whole) and the *market vortex*. A market wedge is a slice in price and time of the whole, and a vortex is the point where a pattern is similar in multiple time frames (for example, the daily pattern is similar to the weekly, or the 30-minute price pattern is similar to the daily). It is a moment when the market is centered and forces are at their greatest to spring into a change of direction.

The Market Wedge

With a market wedge, a shorter time frame goes against the greater time series preceding it. The shorter-term traders are moving opposite to the long-term investors (or better yet, against the prevailing trend and forces of the market). Think about it like this: We can have a prevailing trend of an ocean tide going in or going out. It is a force we cannot change or successfully fight. The prevailing tide absolutely rules the direction. Yet with each approaching and receding wave of the ocean, we can safely time our jump into the water. With a tide moving in against us, we can enter against the prevailing forces of the tide by running into the water as the wave recedes, allowing the pull of the wave to bring us into the water. This is successful even though the tide is really going against us. When we are in the water and the tide is rapidly going out against us (which can be quite

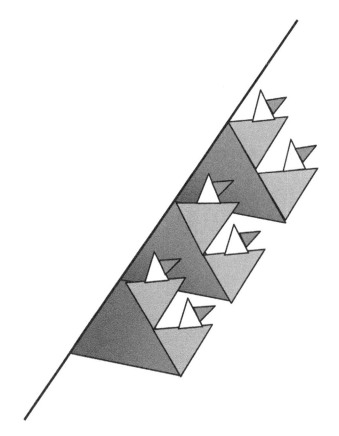

FIGURE 5.5 Market Wedge Concept

dangerous), we can get back onto the beach on a wave, counter to the prevailing tide, heading to the shore. We allow the wave to carry us in.

Figure 5.5 illustrates the concept of the primary trend (tide), and shows the waves that create the complete structure and are the parts of the whole. In markets, the prevailing forces of the economy (even those not yet seen) drive the dominant trend. And just as in the tides of the ocean, this can be invisible to those watching each wave. These forces will ultimately move all tribes (market participants) more greatly than any single group. Yet following this primary force are the counter-waves or slices that are essential to the whole. And below this, ever smaller counter-waves (ripples, if you will). Each of these wave levels conceptualized in Figure 5.5 represents a separate time period. And in each period, there are different motivations driving the participants. Just as a day trader is not concerned with the larger forces of economic shifts, nor is the spread trader concerned with the concerns of the day trader. Each wave, or price pattern fractal, reflects

FIGURE 5.6 U.S. Long Bond Future Contract, Monthly Since 1985, Non-Log
Source: Genesis Financial Technologies, Inc.

the strongest participants of its time period. As in nature, there are no straight lines. There must be counter-moves to support the entire set.

Figure 5.6 demonstrates a primary trend where the whole of the pattern of the prices of U.S. Long Bond is in one direction. This chart is a picture of the ongoing economic shifts in the economy over the past 25 years. Looking at it, you might conclude that all one needs to do is simply hold onto bonds and be a winner. In the real world, though, the long *buy-and-hold* strategy is costly and impractical. It is no different than the swimmer from our preceding example of the tides saying he will stand in one spot until the tide comes in and still be able to go swimming. If he were to stand in one spot all day, he might wind up baking in the sun waiting for the water, or drowning in the depths of the water as the tide rises over him. For an investor, buy-and-hold would be just as absurd a premise, resulting in ruin.

Let's look at a smaller part of the whole in Figure 5.7. This may be a wave we can ride ashore.

Where is the trend? Obviously it is down. We see lower lows and lower highs. Yet, are we thinking about the exact same market as in Figure 5.6? What about more recently in 2006 and 2007 in Figure 5.8?

Each of these figures represents monthly or weekly periods of significant downtrends in a multi-decade period of ever-decreasing interest rates

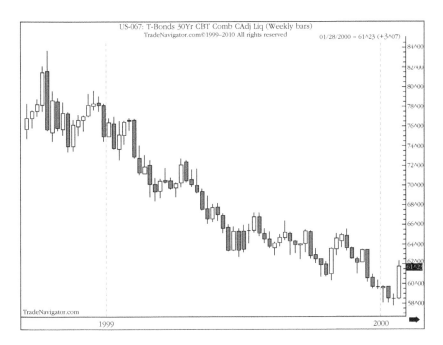

FIGURE 5.7 U.S. Long Bond, Future, between 1999 and 2000
Source: Genesis Financial Technologies, Inc.

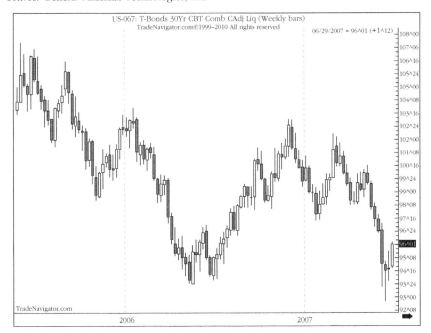

FIGURE 5.8 U.S. Long Bond, Future, between 2006 and 2007
Source: TradeNavigator.com.

and increasing bond prices. A *long-only* strategy would suffer considerable periods of extreme negative returns, rendering it an impossible strategy to sustain; but let's take a closer look at the shorter time periods during these corrections against the now-multi-decade bull market in the U.S. Long Bond. What happens when we look at the smaller wedges of time of the whole set of price data? Counter to the multi-decade bull trend seen in Figure 5.6, Figures 5.7 and 5.8 show down wedges against the primary trend.

What would be a realistic trading approach? Think back to the illustrations in Figure 5.6. This can be easily done using a semi-log representation (which one should do when plotting the progression of a very long data series). Then plot the fractal order of the price structure onto Figure 5.6, or Figure 5.9, which considers the log scale of price.

In Figures 5.10 and 5.11, we then break down price to the daily and intraday time periods using the same method for the wedges of price structure.

FIGURE 5.9 U.S. Long Bond, Monthly, Log Scale
Source: Genesis Financial Technologies, Inc.

FIGURE 5.10 U.S. Long Bond, Daily
Source: Copyright 2010 Bloomberg Finance LP.

FIGURE 5.11 U.S. Long Bond, Daily, 60 Minutes, Intraday
Source: Copyright 2010 Bloomberg Finance LP.

ANOTHER REAL-WORLD EXAMPLE   Before we leave the idea of the market wedge with fractal slices that move counter to the preceding price waves, or primary trend, let's examine an equity that can be proxy for the overall economies of North America and Europe: Dell, Inc.

As we see in Figure 5.12, Dell has been in a multiyear downtrend since the reversal and market shift of 2000 (which was preceded by enormous periods of relative momentum and price volatility). The chart is a picture of receding forces in the economy.

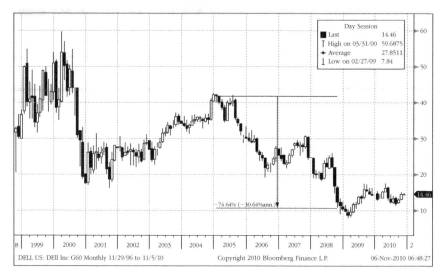

FIGURE 5.12 Dell Inc., 1999–2010
Source: Copyright 2010 Bloomberg Finance LP.

Dell was a terrific investment between 1996 and 1999 but has been a poor investment for the past 10 years, losing more than 75 percent of its value in this time period. Yet when we look closer at the price behavior of this same stock and within this time period on a weekly scale between October 2001 and October 2004, it more than doubled in value, with a 34 percent annualized return. What a great time that was to invest in Dell (see Figure 5.13).

As we see by the examples above, in general, we can build a trading method around the concept of market wedges. But, there is another application of fractal wave patterns of price.

The Market Vortex: Clarity and Power

The market vortex can be defined as the moment when multiple scales of time and cycles come together and are one, drawing us in a single direction. The market vortex is the center of the dominant forces on price, pointing to a market shift of the foremost magnitude (see Figure 5.14). This is when markets as visualized in multiple time periods—monthly, weekly, daily, and intraday—point us in the same direction of the absolute forces on the market shift, or change. Regardless of the time frame, the pattern repeats. When this

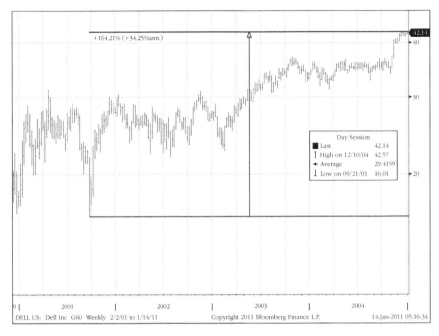

FIGURE 5.13 Dell, October 2000–January 2005
Source: Copyright 2010 Bloomberg Finance LP.

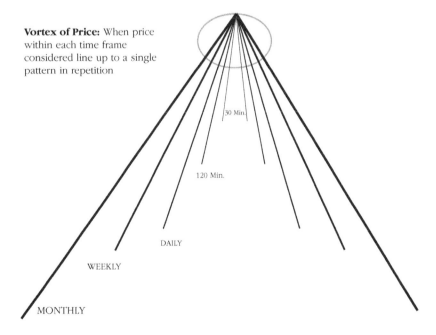

FIGURE 5.14 Illustration of a Vortex

happens, an *Elliottician* (an adherent to Elliott Wave theory) might classify it the confluence of the fifth wave in all cycles. We can call this the *price vortex*.

The idea of a price vortex, or a point of shift, is a conceptual foundation of *wave and fractal market theory*. But rather than conducting ever-changing wave counts or applying fractal diffusion equations to measure the rate of change of price data, how can we practically capture this idea in our everyday decision making and work as traders?

Unlike fractal pattern slices, where we observe waves of price movement counter to the previous level of price trend, the vortex of price is observed when indications of a trend shift are repeated simultaneously in multiple time frames as conceptualized in the illustration in Figure 5.14.

RETURNING TO DELL   Let's return to Dell as it entered a vortex. See Figure 5.15.

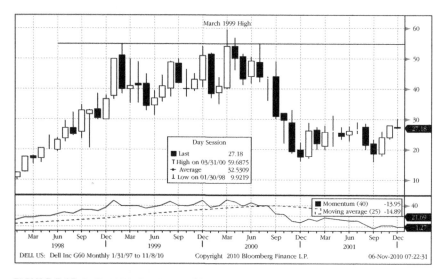

FIGURE 5.15 Dell, 1999–2000, Monthly
Source: Copyright 2010 Bloomberg Finance LP.

Briefly and simply, we have a new high in March 2000 where the close of the month is at or below ⅓ of the high of the complete price bar. (Note that, we also have relatively extreme momentum.) In addition to price rejection of the probe beyond former highs, this action alerts us to a *potential* weakening in the market. The trend remains up with the prevailing tide still in one direction. However, against a weak monthly close and volatility after this new high, observant analysts and investors are now warned that there is a storm brewing with a mix of volatility, an extreme in momentum, and a relatively weak monthly close. Conditions are changing, at least for now. We see that a market shift and a movement of the dominant tribe are under way.

Upon this monthly signal, we now reduce our time scale to the weekly period from the end of February to April and observe the pattern of this reversal warning month in the shorter time scale, as appears in Figure 5.16. After a rapid run-up to test old highs, the market sold off over the next weeks.

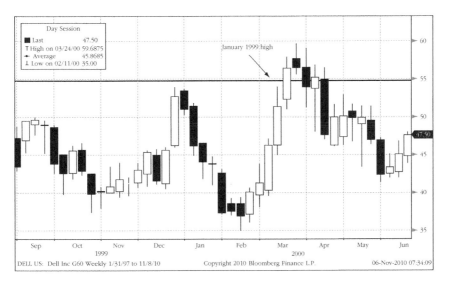

FIGURE 5.16 Dell Inc., 1999–2000, Weekly
Source: Copyright 2010 Bloomberg Finance LP.

We see in the week of March 24 that there was a new weekly high with a close below the open. While (at that time and in the real world) the monthly reversal pattern had not yet revealed itself we had a weekly reversal in this slice of the time period. For the short-term trader and investor, this poor weekly close was an alert to close out positions (or, for directional equity traders, to go short).

Let's break down the price action time frame even further. What does the daily price action and pattern of that week tell us? Figure 5.17 shows us a pattern giving us the exact same message. As we see, this new probe higher is met with price rejection and resistance. So, observing this, we've determined serious price rejection is now coming into the market.

On March 22, 2000, Dell saw its all-time high at almost 60.00 per share with a close near the bottom of the day. This price action on its own, as before, does not tell much. Yet for the short-term trader observing the daily action, and the intraday trader, this move gave a message. It was a day to be short. The next day was a day to sell. In turn, the entire week was a selling week at this failed probe beyond previous price highs of January 1999.

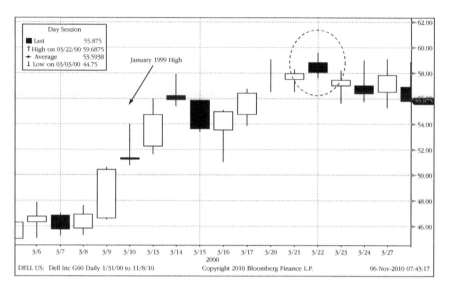

FIGURE 5.17 Dell Inc., March 2000, Daily
Source: Copyright 2010 Bloomberg Finance LP.

FIGURE 5.18 Dell Inc., March–April 2000, Daily
Source: Copyright 2010 Bloomberg Finance LP.

Over the next trading sessions, the intraday attempts to return and exceed resistance at this now-key level were immediately rejected by the market, giving us the negative close seen in Figure 5.18. Over the next weeks, the market established price zones of ever-lower rejection and acceptance with minor rallies in very short time scales. There was an undertow, and the direction of the tide was shifting from going higher to lower. Higher prices were repeatedly rejected as observed here in multiple time frames—monthly, weekly, daily, and intraday. The low-risk opportunities to sell were now against the minor waves up. While the month of March 2000 put in new highs as it tested the recent highs, it closed significantly off the highs of the month, giving us a monthly reversal down. Within this month, the daily and intraday wedges of price were in a downtrend as higher prices were repeatedly rejected by market participants.

Against the backdrop of the two-period monthly reversal pattern seen in Figure 5.15, you can develop a selling or exit strategy on what could be an emerging vortex constellation against the weekly, daily, and intraday price behavior as all periods signal weakness. In this example, we reversed the vortex from the monthly we have observed after the fact, down to the weekly, daily, and intraday time slices, which revealed to us repeated price rejection in multiple time frames. A look at the smaller wedges of the pattern revealed something the whole (the longer-term chart pattern) didn't exactly tell us. The smaller wedges revealed the true changing nature of the market: The dominant tribes were breaking apart and the market was shifting direction.

Recognizing this ongoing shift from the monthly and weekly closing prices, a strategy would be to break the time scale down into shorter periods and then identify levels of price acceptance and rejection. Conceptualizing and visualizing that each of the wedges, or waves, are counter to the new prevailing tide, a trading strategy could be to sell into a wave counter to the new tide down

A Spin in the Opposite Direction

Let's look at the vortex from the other direction—inside out—as might now be unfolding.

Figure 5.19 shows new daily highs in the 30-year Bond on August 18, 2010, which were probed and rejected over the next trading sessions. On September 1, the market opened gap lower and sold off all day. The market then sold off over the next sessions to be met with buying at the support range just below 130-00.

This is seen more clearly in the intraday action in Figure 5.20 between October 6 and 12, where the second probe to recent highs (as identified in Figure 5.19) were rejected. Short-term traders are alerted to this repeated price rejection. This pattern can be extrapolated into the visualization of a possible reversal. Based on this, our strategy can sell into each rejection bar.

Moving out from this period, into the weekly shown in Figure 5.21, we observe an extremely sharp (in this case) reversal, initiating a possible

FIGURE 5.19 U.S. Long Bond, Future, Daily
Source: Copyright 2010 Bloomberg Finance LP.

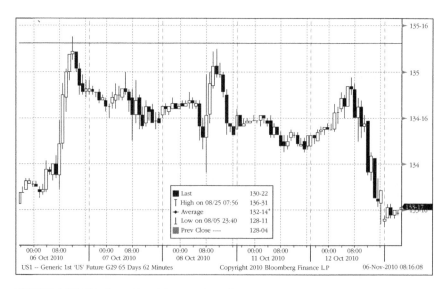

FIGURE 5.20 U.S. Long Bond, Future, Intraday
Source: Copyright 2010 Bloomberg Finance LP.

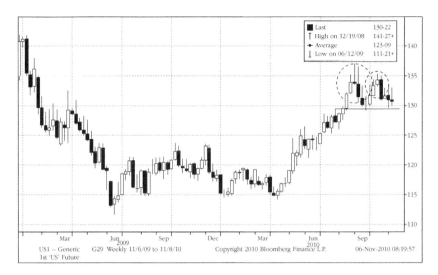

FIGURE 5.21 U.S. Long Bond, Future, Weekly
Source: Copyright 2010 Bloomberg Finance LP.

new wave down. It is an outward extension of the pattern unfolding in
the shorter timeframes preceding this weekly pattern.

When you look at all three figures together, the monthly pattern is a
continued extension of the weekly, the weekly pattern of the daily, and the
daily pattern of the intraday. The bond market, which sold off for weeks
and months in this case, is currently in the phase of a counter-wave to what
appears to be the ongoing tidal shift in the credit market that kicked off in
late 2009. If we are indeed in the vortex of change, as this unfolding pattern
seems to indicate, the continued lowering of interest rates is soon to be
behind us.

Conclusion

It can be a paradox. The appropriate adage would be: "We cannot see the
forest for the trees." This is what happens when we observe only the small
picture (as in looking at a shorter time period of price action). When we
do this, we can lose sight of what is happening in the big picture. But it
really is only by carefully observing the shorter-term or granular price action
that we detect disturbances in the primary trend and see the emergence
of shifts in the markets.

As market observers, it is critical to our success to understand price
action in all time frames and under multiple conditions. This is the lesson
of similarity or repeating order as well as the fractal dimension of natural

systems, including financial markets. A trader can use low-risk trading strategies to get positioned for a market change using the concepts of primary trend and secondary counter-trends, and fractal wedges for trade setups and entry.

With the tools introduced in this chapter, we can now consider the next and larger fractal pattern: *the Valley of the Kings.*

CHAPTER 6

Into the Valley of the Kings and the Place of Truth

Pattern Concepts to Enter a Market on the Run

Don Quixote sighted a man riding towards them with something on his head that shone as if it were made of gold, and as soon as he saw this man he turned to Sancho and said, "It appears to me, Sancho, that there is no proverb which is not true, because they are all maxims derived from experience itself, the mother of all knowledge: especially one that says, 'when one door closes, another opens.'"

—*The Ingenious Hidalgo Don Quixote de la Mancha*
by Miguel de Cervantes Saavedra. [Translated by John Rutherford,
Penguin Books, London (2003), p. 166.]

In previous chapters we covered market conditions and patterns behind major change. Some might consider the approaches discussed as countertrend strategies. *Countertrend* is an expression that rings of going against the market instead of capturing change—which is the essence of speculation and investment. What about considering pattern-based strategies to position oneself into ongoing change, or an upward "trend-continuation" strategy? This is what we call patterns such as the *Valley of the Kings* and the *Place of Truth*. But first, a little background on the concepts behind these patterns.

About 50 kilometers south of Cairo, Egypt, in a narrow valley on the west bank of the Nile River, lies the Valley of the Kings, where the Theban Tombs were built over centuries between around 2500 and 1000 B.C. The tombs were built for the Egyptian Pharaohs, nobles, scribes, and the most skilled and honored craftsmen. There is only one entrance into the valley, which is a long narrow path (narrow as it provided protection for the tombs). During the second dynastic period of Egypt (before the Great Pyramids were built) the valley was a secret and the entrance was well-guarded to protect the tombs from plunder. The tombs range from simple pit-like structures to one with an elaborate maze of over 121 chambers.[1] In 1922, King Tutankhamen was discovered here, and while that may be the most famous and glamorous find, it did not tell us much more than we already knew about ancient Egyptian culture and artistry.

The Valley of the Kings remains the richest archeological site in the world and excavations continue to this day. But there is another region in the valley, less well known in the popular imagination, and where the most informative remains of ancient culture and everyday life can be found. It is named the "Place of Truth," called *Set Maat* in 2000 B.C., and is just south of the Theban Tombs (in an area now called Deir el Medina). The Place of Truth was home to the most highly skilled craftsmen, artisans, and their families. They were called "Servants in the Place of Truth" and built the incredibly magnificent tombs for the royals in the Valley of the Kings. Those who lived in the Place of Truth had a most privileged and protected existence.

Yet when most of us think about the tombs of kings in Egypt we think of the Pyramids of Giza. These, however, came much later. The royal tombs cut into the limestone in the Valley of the Kings, which were built much earlier than those in Giza, followed an even simpler royal cemetery. The tombs of this even earlier period (called the Old Kingdom) were rectangular, flat-topped constructions with sloping sides called *mastaba* (after the Arabic word for benches).[2] In fact, it is thought that the origin of this structure goes back to prehistoric times when mud-brick and rubble mounds covered subterranean pit graves. The more elaborate forms of the *mastaba* (see Figure 6.1) had an offering space built in that had a false door on the western wall. This door represented the symbolic crossing point between the physical world and the spiritual world, and the idea of a continuation of life beyond.

This form (see Figure 6.1) is thought to have been a symbol of the primeval hill that emerged out of the waters of chaos from which the Creator brought forth life and order. So this, and later the Pyramids (said to be a manifestation of the rays of the sun), are symbols of the "resurrection of the human remains protected beneath it."[3]

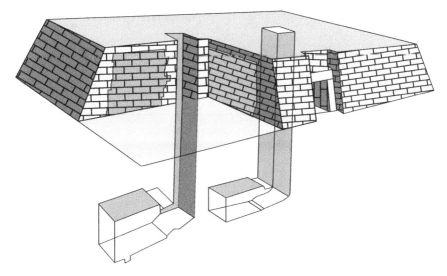

FIGURE 6.1 Mastaba Tomb Form
Source: Koen van der Ahé, http://commons.wikimedia.org

The Valley of the Kings in Equities

Since our concern is the markets, what does the Valley of the Kings and the Place of Truth have to do with modern markets and pattern visualization? The symbolism of these places gives us a way of thinking about a phase of market price action: continuation and order emerging out of chaos; a regeneration; an escape from the confines of a "box" to continue the path on a long journey. In trading, the Valley of the Kings is a market condition we can define and recognize to give us a pattern. As traders and investors, we want to be on the alert for the times when a market with an established direction enters into a "valley" or a place for regeneration. We will observe the distinguishing patterns of markets in the phase of the Valley of the Kings, and the order this gives to a market, and a phase we can act on.

Importantly, the Valley of the Kings phase is an uptrend-continuation pattern. It can appear after a clear trend has exerted itself. In terms of our previous metaphor, it occurs when price returns to the valley to regain strength before it is reborn and continues its journey through the western door and out to the Beyond. Recognizing this continuation pattern gives us an opportunity to add, enter, or reenter a market during the regenerative phase and before it continues on its upward path. It is an anticipatory pattern and is represented in Figure 6.2.

The deepest part of the valley is in the basin of a bear leg down (or counter-wedge) of a market that has seen a sustained bull run. This is where the market goes for its rebirth. As we will see in the following

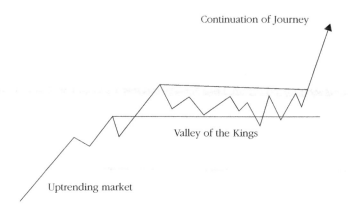

FIGURE 6.2 Valley of the Kings Pattern Concept: Uptrending Healthy Market to the Upside, with Entering Valley of Price for Regeneration and Rebirth

examples, the valley can be deep, narrow, time consuming, and difficult to pass. The price range may be wide. There may be what appear to be "false breakouts" with price action oscillating between the wide price range of support and resistance (S&R), or phases of little price movement over longer periods of time.

It's important to remember that the valley is not specifically a trade setup, but instead a state of the market where we can seek our own trade setup. I describe it here in general terms using very simple indicators to detect the market pattern condition so you are alerted to it and can then use your own tools to navigate and possibly act on it. To apply, for example, an entry strategy to the long side when a secular bull market is in the Valley of the Kings (before it makes its escape out the false door).

Figure 6.2 illustrates the first preconditions for the Valley of the Kings: A market must have had a sustained uptrend, perhaps even a trend that simply "got away" from you. We can easily see this looking at the figure, but to define it, and for simplicity and purposes of illustration, I limit it to measuring a trend with standard trend line analysis (higher highs and lower lows) and a 40-period *exponential moving average (EMA)*. Here, the market must be above its 40-period EMA and well above the longer 200-period EMA (which is accepted as a sustained uptrend by most standards and definitions). As the market enters into the valley (Figure 6.3) it breaks to the downside below the 40-period EMA.

To remain a denizen of the royal kings, this market may not sustain a break below, for example, the 200-period EMA, or key long-term price support ranges as determined by S&R price cluster zones. When in the valley, the market then enters an oscillating phase where one sees repeated patterns of bull and bear flags. The market moves back and forth within the Valley of the Kings during this stage of rejuvenation. When looking at equities, I first apply these simple indicators just mentioned to the weekly time period. Figure 6.3 and Figure 6.4 illustrate two equities that made repeated visits into the valley.

FIGURE 6.3 TEVA Pharmaceutical Industries Ltd., Weekly: The Big View with Valleys Identified

Source: Copyright 2010 Bloomberg Finance LP.

Teva Pharmaceutical Industries, Ltd. (TEVA) is a major Israeli manufacturer of generic drugs. The equity is listed in multiple exchanges and included in bio-tech indexes, and traded as American Depositary Shares (ADRs) on the U.S. NASDAQ. TEVA can be thought of as a proxy for the global pharmaceutical industry. Another global equity, and somewhat related to the pharmaceutical industry, is Stericycle, Inc. (SRCL), which services waste treatment for the medical industry in the Americas, Argentina, and the U.K. and Ireland.

Both of these companies are major players in industries that, considering the aging populations in western economies, remain on a continued secular rising trend. This trend and overall outperformance is easy enough to eyeball from the long-term historical charts in Figures 6.3 and 6.4. We

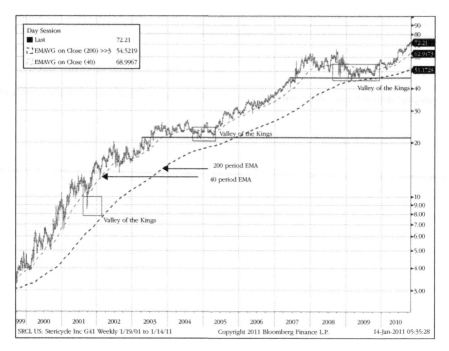

FIGURE 6.4 Stericycle Inc., Weekly: The Big View with Valley Identified
Source: Copyright 2010 Bloomberg Finance LP.

can now easily identify the regeneration phase when each entered into the
Valleys of the Kings (see the weekly charts depicted in Figures 6.3 and 6.4).

What are the six overall characteristics of the Valley of the Kings seen
in Figures 6.3 and 6.4?

1. The market experienced a sustained uptrend within the period
   considered.
2. Price makes multiple breaks and probes below the 40-period EMA (or
   any numerically based indicator; the indicator is not an absolute, but
   an *indication*).
3. The market sells off to enter the Valley of the Kings, where the deepest
   point of the valley is very often (but not always) previous key resistance
   during the uptrend phase.
4. The market remains above the 200–250-period EMA.
5. During the rejuvenation phase, price oscillates between support and
   resistance areas of the valley.
6. The end phase of the valley is an "escape-like" rapid exit, indicated
   by decisive price action to the upside.

A Closer Look at the Place of Truth

Let's zoom into a closeup of a valley to see the dynamics of price action inside of it. Readers of the previous chapters immediately recognize in both Figures 6.3 and 6.4 the dynamics of a price rejection (and support) often at or around the 200-period EMAs as price is in the valley below the 40-period MA.

With a closer look (see Figure 6.5), we now move to a shorter time frame and into the Place of Truth. We carefully observe here how the real work of the market is being done during the regeneration phase. Important for a trading approach is to see exactly how the condition of price action is constructed. From this, we can visualize, plan, and build an orderly trading strategy.

FIGURE 6.5 Zoom of Weekly Chart of TEVA Valley, October 2008–May 2009
Source: Copyright 2010 Bloomberg Finance LP.

Figures 6.5 and 6.6 illustrate that over a period of a few short days, TEVA crashed into the Valley of the Kings. The daily chart (Figure 6.6) illustrates the break and descent into the valley as priced gapped down below the 40 and 200 daily EMA after testing and failing at the S&R line.

Candlestick pattern aficionados will recognize the *doji* of October 10, in Figure 6.6, adding another element to the entire pattern. On the doji

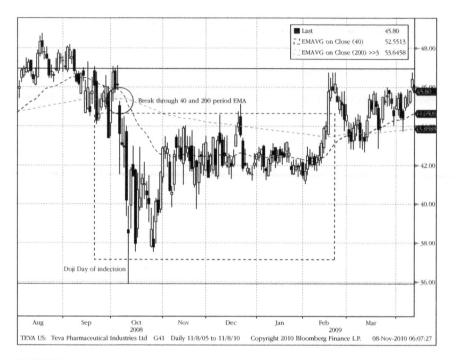

FIGURE 6.6 Zoom of Daily Chart of TEVA Valley, October 2008–May 2009
Source: Copyright 2010 Bloomberg Finance LP.

day, the deepest point at the basin of the valley met buying and price rejections of lows at previous resistance. The action on this day tells us that the bears are beginning to lose control of that sell off and there is now indecision. Following this sell off and rejection of lower prices, the market oscillated within the valley for three months (gaining strength) until it made its decisive escape during the week of February 20.

As seen by the weekly overview chart (Figure 6.7), SRCL was trending down from the highs of 2008 with multiple short-term probes below the 40-week EMA. The nature of price regeneration is seen in Figure 6.8.

Here we see a similar pattern construction and price dynamic. In the week of February 20, the market entered a low and attempted to breach the 200-period weekly EMAs to be met with strong rejection of lower prices. Over the next weeks and months, the market oscillated inside the Valley of the Kings, yet with higher highs and lower lows as a classic bullish trend channel unfolded. Figure 6.7 shows something characteristic for the Valley of the Kings pattern: The market made a reversal up out of the valley (the weekly S&R Range) to escape and continue its journey to the upside.

Let's look at the daily price action during this rejuvenation (see Figure 6.8).

FIGURE 6.7 SRCL Valley, Weekly Closeup
Source: Copyright 2010 Bloomberg Finance LP.

FIGURE 6.8 SRCL Valley, Daily, April 2008–December 2008
Source: Copyright 2010 Bloomberg Finance LP.

Again, we see in Figure 6.8 the classic dynamics of lower price rejection while the market dwells in the valley. This signals the trader to a potential opportunity, based on a clear trading strategy, to position to the long side before the market makes its rapid exit through the door to the upside as it did in November 2009.

FIGURE 6.9 Schlumberger Ltd. (SLB), Weekly, Valley with Probes below the 40 period EMA
Source: Copyright 2010 Bloomberg Finance LP.

Important to remember when we consider this pattern is that the Valley of the Kings phase often extends over many weeks and months, also seen in Figures 6.9 and 6.10. It is a construct to understand and visualize price action of an ongoing secular bull market. It is a period of rejuvenation and therefore requires time. Trade entry decisions, however, may be built on the shorter-term daily and intraday price dynamics of what we call the Place of Truth when price is in the valley.

The Valley of the Kings in Commodities

Looking to the commodity markets, we consider a similar dynamic but in a shorter time frame. Here the idea is not to enter large secular trends but

FIGURE 6.10 Schlumberger Ltd. (SLB), Daily, Same Period, Valley with Detail of Price Action in the Place of Truth in the Valley
Source: Copyright 2010 Bloomberg Finance LP.

to step in and capture the shorter-term trends lasting up to a few months as seen in many commodities. When a commodity market has entered a sustained and healthy trend phase (one that may last over months), waiting for the entry into the Valley of the Kings phase alerts you to low-risk long-entry trading opportunities.

Corn is the most liquid traded grain market on the largest grain exchange (Chicago Board of Trade) with an average now exceeding well over 300,000 contracts traded daily on the front delivery month. In 2006, Corn kicked off what turned out to be an extended trend going from below 4.80 to over 6.60 per bushel. Shortly after this period of gains, the story of increasing use of biofuels and the threat of increased allocation of food resources to energy entered the news cycle.

Prior to this, a market such as Corn was of little or no interest in the public mind. Suddenly, grain markets were of interest even to those who could not differentiate between a stalk of corn and a soybean pod. Major magazines ran features on the threat of our daily food being used for energy—that, for example, the first world would power their SUVs at the expense of food for the third world. Everything from commodity funds to

ETFs on renewable commodities such as Corn and Wheat, and even Cotton, emerged as investment vehicles for everyone. The world was suddenly sold the story of investing in real assets by buying corn and soybeans. How could the prudent trader enter this market?

FIGURE 6.11 Weekly Corn from January 2006–January 2008 in the Valley
Source: Copyright 2010 Bloomberg Finance LP.

Figure 6.11 illustrates Corn kicking off its strong multi-week rally, to then almost as quickly sell off and enter into a phase of regeneration below the 40 period EMA (the phase we call the Valley of the Kings). The observant trader following the Corn market, or suddenly finding interest in Corn, may have sensed an opportunity. Why?

In Figure 6.12, showing the daily price action of this period, there is a characteristic pattern revealing the truth of the sell-off where price orients around the previous range of resistance. As we see, lower prices are rejected and the area of regeneration and accumulation displays a textbook bull wedge of higher highs and lower lows as price oscillates within the Place of Truth.

FIGURE 6.12 Daily Corn from June 2006–December 2008 in the Valley
Source: Copyright 2010 Bloomberg Finance LP.

In the Valley for the Short-Term Commodity Trader

Most commodity traders are extremely short term relative to equities and interest rate products. Actively traded commodity futures contracts exist for hedging and risk transfer and speculative participants provide needed liquidity to these markets.

The same concept of the Valley of the Kings can be also applied to methods for the very short-term trader. In July 2010, Soybeans started to charge north. Primary drivers of this move were (as is usual at this time of year) weather-related. Figure 6.13 depicts the minor and short-lived pullbacks to below the 40-period EMA and—characteristically—to previous short-term resistance, which was now price support. For the aggressive short-term trader looking for an entry into the market, this is your Place of Truth, allowing a relatively low-risk entry.

Beyond that, we can see the market has since moved another 10 cents, allowing opportunity somewhere in that range for the nimble trader seeking to go long in the direction of this primary trend (in July 2010).

Update: The price action of July portended that Soybeans was entering a new trend, and it did, indeed, become a king once again. Figure 6.14

FIGURE 6.13 Soybeans, Daily
Source: Copyright 2010 Bloomberg Finance LP.

FIGURE 6.14 Soybeans, Daily, Summer–Fall 2010
Source: Copyright 2010 Bloomberg Finance LP.

illustrates a new opportunity to enter to the long side as the market entered a pattern, meeting the conditions of the Valley of the Kings.

Summary

The Valley of the Kings is a conceptual visualization approach for entering a market when the identified market or "king" is in a phase of rejuvenation and rebirth before its upward trend continues. The defining characteristics of this market include an established strongly trending price (regardless of the time frame under consideration) that then enters into a relatively significant decline, and ultimately, the valley. Within the valley is the Place of Truth where the market enters into a period of a oscillation pattern. This is often a narrow price range of S&R. The nature of the price decline is not considered. It can be a slow, gradual, or a sudden sell off. While in the valley, a careful look at the characteristic price action (support/resistance levels and price acceptance/rejection ranges as covered in previous chapters) reveals the patterns of regeneration and increasing price strength until the market makes its escape again on its journey ahead.

Overall, it is a method of visualization to recognize and increase sensitivity to the dynamics behind the unfolding price action after a market break. It is, very simply, a cycle of occurrences that can be summed up as death, rejuvenation, and rebirth. With a picture of the nature of the unfolding market as it enters into each of these phases, we can develop our plan of action around the conditions, personal trading styles, and investing objectives.

Before we leave this pattern, let's return to TEVA in Figure 6.15, where it appears to have once again entered into the valley. The chart shows multiple time frames.

TEVA has broken down from the highs of March 2010 to sell off into the depths of the valley, which is the previous resistance range of 2008. The market is in a current short-term downtrend, but remains above its 200-period EMA.

A closer look at the daily view of the valley more clearly illustrates that we are at a key price area of long-term support and resistance. Figure 6.15 illustrates this possible low point, or *basin* of the valley.

Viewing Figure 6.16 to zoom into the daily chart of TEVA on July 30, 2010, we see that buying came in at the key price level as identified in the weekly and daily charts. In fact, TEVA was the most active equity pre-market trading on that day around these very levels, up 2.88 percent in the pre-market. As TEVA did not have short interest of note to fuel a short-covering rally, it is likely that the long-term value investors moved into the market. (Around the time of this writing, there was no specific news to prompt the buying, yet we had strong buying as I covered TEVA on that day.) Its price has moved into the valley, offering an opportunity

FIGURE 6.15 TEVA, Weekly: **Currently in the Valley**
Source: Copyright 2010 Bloomberg Finance LP.

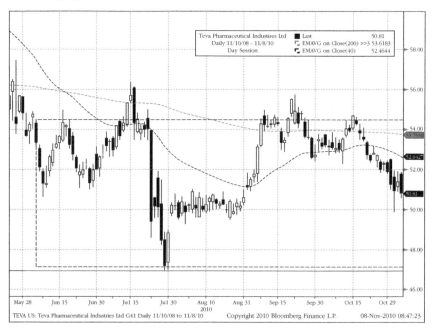

FIGURE 6.16 TEVA, Daily Valley: A Closer Look
Source: Copyright 2010 Bloomberg Finance LP

to market participants. Will the valley be narrow and steep, or will it have a broad basin stretching out over many weeks and months? Of course, we do not know right now. If an equity such as TEVA were on your purchase list coming out of this market condition and unfolding pattern, we could build a trading strategy around this current price action and pattern.

Conclusion

One of the conundrums for most traders is how to enter a trend (or board a train) already on the move. This chapter has taken an unorthodox view of this question and given us a way to think about devising our own trading strategy for a market in this phase. As it is, with a clear conception of the market condition and a defined trading strategy, we can more easily enter the market without our emotions (fear of missing the move, for example) taking control of our trade management.

To build a trading strategy, we can take the ideas and patterns behind the Valley of the Kings and the associated Place of Truth, we can apply standard indicators (such as the use of a 200-period EMA, or a shorter-period EMA for commodity markets) and our understanding of the more orthodox methods of pattern recognition (such as ascending triangle break-outs, expanding tops, asymmetric tops, etc.).

Finally, when using derivatives of price (such as moving averages or any trend measurement) there are no absolute rules. Experiment with rules that fit your trading style and objectives and the character of the underlying market.

Moving from the Valley of the Kings and Place of Truth, we can next examine the specific market conditions and patterns I call *Thunder Before the Storm*. Unlike the Valley of the Kings, the Thunder Before the Storm is brief and happens suddenly with little or no warning. The occurrence of Thunder Before the Storm marks an upheaval as strong as a sudden rumble in the sky before a cloudburst or the rapid increase of wind before a swell in the tides. In short, the Thunder Before the Storm warns us of a major change.

CHAPTER 7

Market Weather

The Quiet before the Storm and the Lightning Bolt—Patterns Signaling an Unexpected Move

"Look here sir," replied Sancho, "withdrawing isn't running away, and waiting isn't prudent when danger outweighs hope, and the wise man saves himself for tomorrow and doesn't risk everything in one day."
—The Ingenious Hidalgo Don Quixote de la Mancha by Miguel de Cervantes Saavedra. [Translated by John Rutherford, Penguin Books, London (2003), p. 187.]

In the previous chapter we covered a continuation pattern and strategies to enter into an existing and well-established trend. What about the trends that take off with a sudden flash from out of nowhere, catching most of us by surprise? What are some of the patterns that define this and how can we trade them?

There is currently a great deal of reporting—for those who follow science news—of the lack of solar activity on the sun. Sun spots and associated solar storm activities have practically disappeared in recent years. There are few solar flares and almost no storm activity. The sun is quiet. In fact, NASA writes, it is "like the quiet before a storm."[1]

Exactly when the storm is expected to arrive remains a topic of debate among scientists. There is concern because everyday life is much more dependent on global electronics than it was almost 50 years ago (the most

133

recent phase of frequent solar storms). At that time, our globe was not surrounded by satellites, nor were we as interconnected by way of mobile communications and the Internet.

Solar storms and major flares have been recorded over the centuries. The most recent major storms occurred in the 1950s, where the solar lights could be seen as far south as Mexico. Future solar storms are disconcerting because they would likely wreak havoc in our atmosphere, resulting in large costs to global economies. But, as I said, for now, things remain very quiet as we wait.

The Quiet before the Storm

We don't have to worry about solar storms right now, but what about the everyday "quiet before the storm" right here on Earth—the one most of us have experienced that happens subtly and suddenly? When a storm is approaching, birds stop chirping and dogs rise from their slumber and run indoors. The air suddenly becomes still and the first black cloud reaches over the horizon as thick drops of rain begin to pound down. The quiet before the storm is that very brief moment when activity moves along at a normal pace and then everything seems to stop within a second or two of absolute quiet. This is the moment right before the storm hits and rain, thunder, and lightning arrive.

What causes this sensation in the atmosphere? Shortly before a storm, an enormous amount of vapor and heat form an updraft into what will be the center of the storm. We might sense it, but do not actually see this updraft in nature, and so it goes in the markets, too.

An updraft in the atmosphere disperses saturated air in a developing storm system, pushing it over increasingly extended tops of the highest storm clouds. (This is why we often see funnel-like and dramatic heat clouds reaching high into the sky before a storm.) Then, the air starts to descend, making the air warmer and drier. With this, there is a different feel to the air around us due to this descending, yet stable air mass. We sense a change is on the way. And this rapid change in the air mass is what creates the calm you sense before a storm hits. Animals that are more sensitive to atmospheric changes seem to react to this type of change first. So what does this have to do with the markets? The nature metaphor can be drawn toward a conceptualization of price behavior where there are unforeseen forces at work. We can call this conceptualization the *quiet before the storm*.

The quiet before the storm is a signal for traders. Of course, we do not see a lid of descending dry air, but for us, it is the moment when participants feel a change and seem to suddenly close their books, turn off their computers, and make an exit right before the storm hits. Experienced traders can attest to this phenomenon: It is almost as if there is a communal thinking. We see the sudden quiet in price behavior, and we all act similarly and accordingly. (Such a phenomenon can lead us to consider the possibility of global collective consciousness, but that is a separate, and sometimes controversial, topic.)

Now that you have the background to the metaphor, let's review a few examples of this storm price pattern at work.

The Storm in Markets

Many traders are familiar with the *ascending wedge* or *ascending triangle* pattern shown in Figure 7.1. For now, erase what you may have learned about the statistical probabilities of a breakout or the predictive significance of this pattern as we examine it in liquid markets.

From September 2009 to January 2010, Corn trended up, sustaining price above the 40-period daily moving average in September and well above the 200-daily moving average in early November (shown in Figure 7.2). With price established well above two significant moving averages, was this an uptrend?

We learn that when a market is in an uptrend, an ascending wedge will most often break to the upside in the direction of the primary trend, as seen in Figure 7.3. This, and that it is the completion and result of a wedge

FIGURE 7.1 Basic Ascending or Rising Wedge Price Pattern
Source: Copyright 2010 Bloomberg Finance LP.

FIGURE 7.2 Corn in Apparent Bullish Market in Ascending Wedge Pattern
Source: Copyright 2010 Bloomberg Finance LP.

FIGURE 7.3 Spot Gold in Ascending Wedge Pattern with Breakout in Direction of Primary Trend
Source: Copyright 2010 Bloomberg Finance LP.

or triangle pattern, is taught in classic tutorials of price pattern analysis. In fact, in some trading literature, geometric price projections are made based on the length of the triangle as measured from the base of the identified triangle. The classic ascending triangle is a pattern in isolation and outside of the context of the broader ongoing price development (the market atmosphere). The pattern itself is of limited application for consistent successful trading strategies, ergo leading to the oft-discussed *failure patterns*. How can we better analyze this common, but often difficult price pattern?

There are a few methods. The quiet of the price within the wedge— when a market is in a state of updraft, counter to the larger trend—may be our quiet before the storm in the markets and a tip on direction.

When this pattern fails to portend price breaking out in continuation to the upside, it is called a *failure break*. It is called a failure because price did not unfold as expected according to the identified ascending wedge pattern. Price action did not behave as it should. In my mind, this pattern is not a failure at all; instead, under certain market conditions, it is an indicator and an identifiable pattern with predictive potential. This is when the trading world stands still; and there is little or no price movement. It is a market entering the quiet before its storm.

Let's take a larger look at the Corn market in Figure 7.4 and the quiet before its storm.

FIGURE 7.4 CBOT Corn Future: Front Month, Daily Trending up into an Ascending Wedge.

Source: Copyright 2010 Bloomberg Finance LP.

Without much explanation, the pattern in Figure 7.4 should be recognizable to readers of the previous chapters. The extended ascending wedge was the retracement of the break in the summer of 2009. Price retraced to the key levels of the definitive price break on June 15, 2009. The massive price breakdown seen earlier is our conceptual metaphor of the storm clouds on the horizon in the background. Yet standard indicators such as moving averages *confirm* we are in an uptrend (sort of like the sun shining with black clouds on the horizon!).

With a look at the top of the wedge, we see here repeated rejection of price in an increasingly narrow range. There is quiet and indecision. This is where the air became still; there was little trading activity. Looking at the bigger picture we see much more: The price action is a retracement to 4.22, which we also note was the opening price (and range) of the break on June 15, 2009. The price retracement against the larger ongoing trend has removed the dispersed air out of the market (see Figure 7.4).

We never know the exact moment of the downdraft that will cause the cloud to burst. Yet, for a trading approach—and especially when we have supporting reason(s) to enter into a directional trade—the narrow range within the wedge and against the larger retracement pattern may signal the impending storm. This is not a countertrend trade, and unlike the Valley of the Kings pattern (where a market is in a stage of rejuvenation on its way to the *upside*), it is a pattern to capture a trend continuation to the *downside*. It is seen in a market that is negatively charged (in the midst of a larger downtrend) and just about to break down.

Before we continue, please note there is another reason why this pattern would be referred to as a *failure*. In the very short-term candlestick pattern in the upper range of the wedge we see a *bullish engulfing* pattern— where a down day is completely engulfed by the following up day (or price period). This is considered a short-term bullish pattern—another reason to support the idea of an impending breakout to the upside. However, for us, and in consideration of the larger unfolding pattern constellation preceding this pattern, we cannot give much weight to this short-term three-day candlestick pattern.

Figure 7.5 also illustrates that the day following the three-day bullish candlestick pattern is indecisive. In spite of the prior day bullish engulfing pattern, the market is unable to continue with the slight upward momentum seen within the narrow range of the previous three days. The market has now gone quiet. With a weak opening on December 1, the trader is given the signal that the wedge has failed, or rather that this was, indeed, our quiet before the storm. We can now make a trading plan against this pattern, going short during the quiet days in anticipation of the breakdown or selling into the break—whatever best fits your trading style and comfort zone.

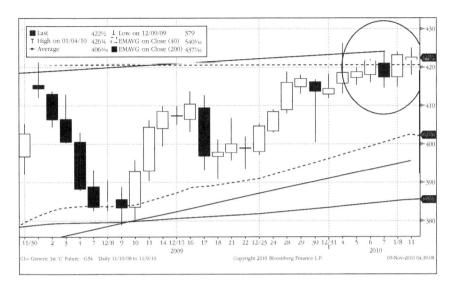

FIGURE 7.5 CBOT Corn Future: Front Month, Daily. Entering Quiet Trading Sessions at Top Range of Wedge.
Source: Copyright 2010 Bloomberg Finance LP.

Considering this pattern in total, the market had not only revealed its real direction, but with techniques using simple pattern recognition, revealed the price point of the break. See Figure 7.6.

FIGURE 7.6 Breakdown of Corn
Source: Copyright 2010 Bloomberg Finance LP.

FIGURE 7.7 Amgen Inc., Long Term
Source: Copyright 2010 Bloomberg Finance LP.

Let's look at an actively traded equity where the quiet before the storm appears and seems to take the market by surprise.

Figure 7.7 shows prices for Amgen, Inc. (AMGN), a manufacturer of human therapeutics. Amgen remains in a long-term downtrend since early 2005. We see this with our eyes and do not need an indicator to confirm this downtrending market characterized by lower highs of peaks and lower lows with each major price swing.

Narrowing in to a shorter time period, we see that in the first days of April 2010, AMGN entered into the ascending wedge pattern with a narrow range (a period of quiet in price action), with price well above its 200-day EMA (see Figure 7.8). With this shorter scale view of this pattern we see the orthodox ascending triangle most often interpreted as a bullish pattern prior to its breakout to the upside. But *is* it bullish? And if not, why not?

When we step back and view this pattern in the context of the entire unfolding pattern constellation, we don't perceive a bullish wedge, but rather something else (see Figure 7.7). We see a market that has made a retracement (an updraft) to the most recent price-rejection range. And here AMGN entered into a wedge of very quiet activity. This is AMGN's quiet before its next storm. This setup allows us to make a low-risk entry into the direction of the primary trend of the market, (short) or to exit longs (see Figures 7.8 and 7.9).

FIGURE 7.8 AMGEN in an Uptrend and Ready to Break up or Down?
Source: Copyright 2010 Bloomberg Finance LP.

FIGURE 7.9 Ascending Wedge Pattern and Predictive Quiet before the Storm
Source: Copyright 2010 Bloomberg Finance LP.

In summary, what we call an ascending wedge may often give the appearance of a market just about to break to the upside. And under some conditions, where the market remains in a healthy primary upward trend this is often the case. However, the pattern must be considered against the longer market condition. A tipoff for the "failure" of this pattern, which is often bearish, is when price enters an updraft (retracement) to a key price area, and we have an ascending wedge where price then enters a narrow range and the action stops.

Looking back to the Spot Gold chart in Figure 7.3, note the nature of price action and preceding market atmosphere before it broke up in contrast to that of Corn or Amgen.

The Lightning Bolt

Many of us have seen lightning bolts on the horizon during a storm, even very nearby, as if from out of the blue. But they are not coming from out of nowhere. Lightning results from complex combinations of built-up atmospheric conditions, just as complex as the combination of atmospheric conditions we discussed before a sudden storm. With lightning, we also never see the conditions for a strike build. In fact, we often see the lightning first and then hear the roll of thunder, and most meteorologists would say that by definition, all thunderstorms contain lightning, whether we see it or not.

Lightning is inherent to thunderstorms. It is simply an invisible electrical discharge in the atmosphere. But the spark of lightning (and this is the pattern we will consider) can unleash a completely new condition. What happens is this (see Figure 7.10): Thunderclouds develop a negative charge at their base, while the ground is positive relative to the cloud. "These electric fields of positive and negative build up, and a huge 'spark' occurs between the cloud and air, or between the cloud and ground."[2] When this large potential difference is discharged, the result is lightning and it begins with an invisible discharge called a *stepped leader*. The leader moves downward in disconnected steps. As this negative leader moves toward the ground, a positive-charge stepped leader moves upward to meet it. It is when these two leaders make contact that visible lightning is seen. We see only the actual strike, but the positive and negative charges creating the strike were always there.

In typical lightning there are down-flowing negative charges; when the positive charges on the ground leap upward to meet them, the jagged downward path of the negative charges lights up with a brilliant flash of light. Because of this, our eyes fool us into thinking that the lightning bolt shoots *down* from the cloud, when in fact the lightning travels *up* from the ground. The visible lightning is called the *return stroke*. So actually

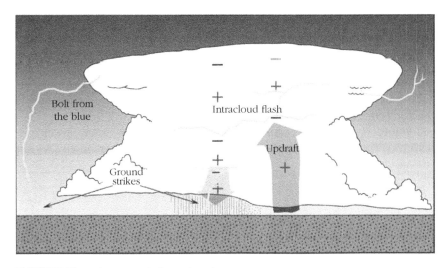

FIGURE 7.10 Lightning Bolt from the Blue

"A typical cloud-to-ground flash is a negative stepped leader that travels downward through the cloud, followed by an upward traveling return stroke. The net effect of this flash is to lower negative charge from the cloud to the ground. Less common, a downward traveling positive leader followed by an upward return stroke will lower positive charge to earth. These positive ground flashes now appear to be linked to certain severe storms and are the focus of intense research by scientists."[3]

Source: National Oceanic and Atmospheric Administration (NOAA).

lightning always comes from below. And this idea is something we can conceptualize and relate to the market price action.

The Lightning Bolt in Markets

What is our lightning pattern in the markets? Do we see it coming beforehand? Is there any warning? Or does it behave just like everyday lightning in that it sometimes strikes far from an actual storm?

The *lightning bolt* pattern in the markets behaves like natural lightning in that markets do become "charged" with competing negative and positive charges in the market atmosphere. We do not see these charges, but a bolt of lightning starts from the meeting of the charges below and moves up, creating a massive "spark" in price and pattern. In the lightning bolt pattern for trading, we are speaking not about a bolt from above, but the bolt from below, just as in nature.

Though getting struck by lightning is extremely rare—I've read it's one chance out of 600,000—there are perhaps hundreds of lightning storms all over the globe at any moment in time. And so it is in the markets.

When we see the bolt of lightning in the markets, it means there is a thunderstorm and a massive change is unfolding. It will be the easiest pattern to detect because it is always identified with certainty after the fact. The bolt has already struck. But, unlike other patterns we have covered, it may be impossible to detect the likelihood of its existence, or the strike, beforehand. By reviewing patterns that show the lightning bolt here, and with more attention to the conditions leading up of the pattern, perhaps traders will be able to discern a method for early warning of the strike. But for now, we can only describe it in its aftermath.

Figure 7.11 depicts Oats trending downward for many weeks in search of value. In this example, the market accepts lower prices. Within

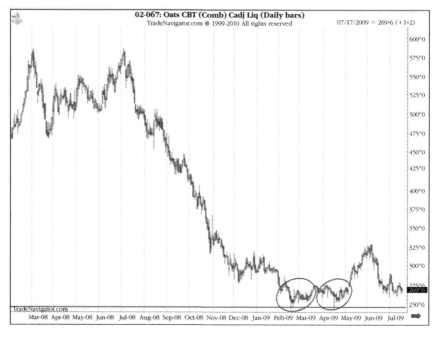

FIGURE 7.11 Oats in a Strong Downtrend
Source: Genesis Financial Technologies, Inc.

this time frame, and with a close examination of the chart, there is no signal to buy going into early summer of 2009. Other than an attempt at "picking a bottom" or buying into what appears to be "oversold," there is absolutely *no* indication to enter into the speculative long side. And as many experienced traders can affirm, *oversold* and *overbought* are relative terms; a market can remain in either condition for a very long period of time as it marches in one direction in search of value.

However, looking at the short-term pattern in May 2010 in Figures 7.12 and 7.13 and leading up to the bolt of lightning, we note a common short-term oscillating action between areas of now-determined support and resistance.

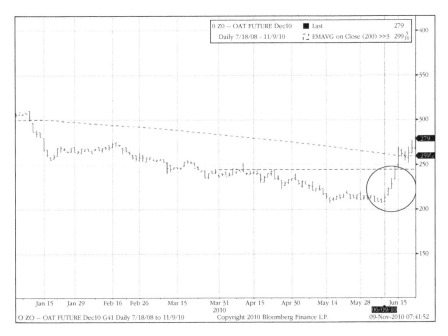

FIGURE 7.12 Oats: Spark in Market as It Is Hit by Lightning (Bar Chart)
Source: Copyright 2010 Bloomberg Finance LP.

While the persistent selling has ceased, there is still surely no change in the downward trend, and nothing to alert anyone but the shortest-term traders in a relatively thin market that is avoided even by many speculative commodity grain traders. (For those who do trade the grain markets, Oats is often followed due to the "Oats indicator"—where Oats may be a leader for the grain complex.)

On June 10, and after three days down but with increasing positive energy building up from below, we have an opening suddenly and unexpectedly well above the close of the previous day. This is the spark of a step leader from below. The next day, on June 11, and after a solid up day where price exceeded the resistance range of the previous five days, the market opens at the high of June 10. In the first minutes of trading, price exceeded the range of the past two weeks to break through the previous resistance range (see Figures 7.12 and 7.13). There is an attracting charge from above and lightning has struck this market. This dynamic is shown in the figures in both bar and candle charts.

The bear market landscape for this commodity is now scorched and we have entered a new market environment. We'll return to strategies on how to enter a market where lightning has struck. But for now, let's first look at the lightning bolt pattern constellation in equities. The chart in Figure 7.14

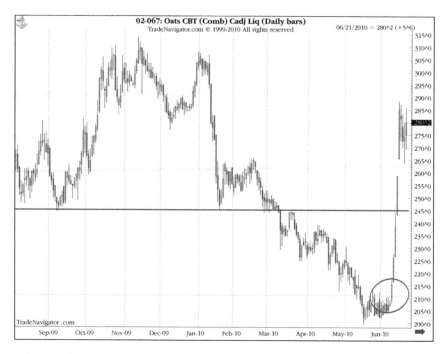

FIGURE 7.13 Oats: Spark in Market as It Is Hit by Lightning (Candle Chart and Strong Bear Trend)
Source: Genesis Financial Technologies, Inc.

shows an actively traded stock we've examined for other patterns: Apple Inc. (AAPL).

As seen in Figure 7.14, during this time AAPL was in a long cyclical downtrend and then entered into an oscillating phase. In the classical technical analysis literature on price patterns, this sort of back-and-forth pattern, as price probes the bands of acceptance and rejection, is called the *accumulation phase*. (In the next chapter we will revisit this chart and see that this pattern is much more than simply an accumulation phase.) Our interest, though, is the precise price pattern as the market is jolted out of this narrow oscillating phase, just as Oats in the previous charts.

In the week of May 7, 2003, Apple was hit by lightning. (In fact, if you have the daily charts going back that far, the exact date of the strike was on May 5.) On that day, and after having been a sleeper on a downward trend—after selling off to new lows in the first weeks of April 2003 and recovering back into the previous support range—the market opened *above* the previous period close to see buying throughout the session and week (see Figure 7.14).

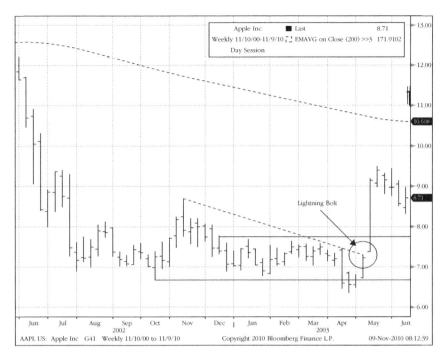

FIGURE 7.14 Apple, Weekly, Lightning Bolt
Source: Copyright 2010 Bloomberg Finance LP.

Features of the Pattern

In the lightning bolt pattern, we have the following three events:

1. An extended downward trend with little or no indication to buy, and surely no change of trend preceding the strike. As seen in the examples, we have a market where a persistent downtrend is scorched into a sudden reverse.
2. Before to the hit, price enters into the most prior support range.
3. The pattern is confirmed as the lightning bolt when the market opens *at* or *above* the previous period close and extends *beyond* current resistance of the S&R range.

A lightning bolt in the markets is rare, but not unknown. And, similar to that in nature, when it does hit, there are consequences. In scanning equities charts for this rare but highly significant lightning bolt pattern, we detect many more instances than initially expected.

FIGURE 7.15 APC: No Buy Signal Here!
Source: Copyright 2010 Bloomberg Finance LP.

Examples of the Lightning Bolt Pattern

Anadarko Petroleum Corp. (APC) is an independent gas-and-oil exploration company with operations in the Americas, Africa, and Asia. Anadarko
had undergone aggressive selling over the previous years. When looking
at Figure 7.15, we find a profitable strategy would be to sell every swing
high. As we see in February 2007, true to the setup for the lightning bolt
pattern, the market was making new lows.

Then by March 21 (see Figure 7.16), price closed at the top of the
previous two-week swing range. Still no real buy signal in a downtrending
market. And, of course we do not see the invisible market step leader that
will initiate the lightning strike.

Then our pattern scan picks up something: In the next trading session,
March 23, *the market opens at the high of the previous session to close up*
for the day and *above* the 40-period EMA. The lightning bolt has struck:
Price closed at the top of an oscillating range. In the following session, the
market opened at or above the high of the previous period. When zeroing
in on short-term price action, identification of price S&R and key levels is
easiest when using candlestick charts.

Like Anadarko, Denbury Resources Inc. (DNR) develops and operates
oil and gas operations, but only in the United States. On April 10, 2007,

FIGURE 7.16 APC: Lightning Strikes!
Source: Copyright 2010 Bloomberg Finance LP.

lightning struck. In Denbury's case, it was after an extended downtrend over a 12-month period, where the market then entered an oscillating phase of over four months with price support, or rejection of lower prices (see Figure 7.17). In Figure 7.18, we again see an accumulation phase before the real strike. (In fact, when looking at the longer-term charts of DNR, we could define this phase as a Valley of the Kings.)

Scanning for the pattern in other sectors, we move out of the often-volatile natural resource and technology-related industries to the rather staid Avery Dennison Corp. (AVY), a manufacturer of office supplies, binders, organizing systems, forms, and similar products. True to the rule, AVY was on a relentless and stunning liquidation move south as it marched in its downtrend path for two years after seeing the highs of January 2007. From the highs of January 2007 and March 2009, AVY lost over 75 percent of its market valuation (see Figure 7.19).

As in previous examples, the strategy of choice would be to sell all minor countertrend rallies as the market sold off in an orderly fashion. The chart of AVY demonstrates a characteristic and crushing liquidation of the equity from many portfolios. From a technical point of view—other than surely oversold indicators flashing at the extreme levels—there was absolutely no hint of an indication to purchase this stock. However, conditions

FIGURE 7.17 DNR in Yearlong Daily Downtrend: No Buy Here for Momentum Traders or Trend Followers!

Source: Copyright 2010 Bloomberg Finance LP.

FIGURE 7.18 DNR Struck by Lightning a Few Days Later

Source: Copyright 2010 Bloomberg Finance LP.

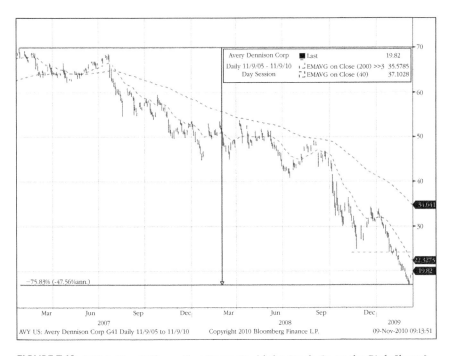

FIGURE 7.19 AVY Selling Off over Two Years: Could the Stock Go to the Pink Sheets?
Source: Copyright 2010 Bloomberg Finance LP.

were building up and a step leader was in force in the atmosphere for this equity. Subsequently, lightning struck, not once, but twice: on April 2, 2009, and April 9, 2009, where the opening price gapped above the range of previous weeks, and *above* the 40-period moving EMA (see Figure 7.20).

In Figure 7.21, we revisit the Corn downtrend after its breakdown from the ascending wedge discussed earlier in this chapter.

Unlike the very brief accumulation phases seen in other markets hit by lightning, Corn made a complete and sudden reversal as it was struck. Here, too, characteristic of the pattern, Corn was in an ongoing and crushing downtrend.

A sudden change is not too unusual in the commodity markets with rapidly changing market-moving information. But then, as we see in Figure 7.22, June 30 had a limit up move of 30 cents after selling off every single day for seven days in a severe leg down. On July 1, and fitting to the conditions of the lightning bolt pattern, we observed the following four events:

1. Corn opened at or above the high range of the previous up-day session.
2. It breached the previous resistance range.

FIGURE 7.20 AVY with the Unusual "V" Bottom Confirmed as Significant Price
Action with the Double Lightning Strike: The World Had Changed for AVY
Source: Copyright 2010 Bloomberg Finance LP.

3. It broke the 40-period exponential moving average (or another of your
   choice).
4. It closed at the top of the recent trading range.

Corn was scorched and something had fundamentally changed. Higher
prices were accepted as the market streamed higher.

Trading the Bolt

We've so far identified where and how lightning hits a market and the
immediate price action following the strike. What's next?

There are multiple approaches to tackling this trading pattern. But before
we go into them, the following charts depict an overview of how markets
unfolded immediately after being struck by lightning (see Figures 7.23
through 7.28). It is never exactly the same, but the lightning bolt portends
a major change and possibly a completely new trend. That is the message
of the pattern.

FIGURE 7.21 CBOT Corn, Daily, 2009–2010
Source: Copyright 2010 Bloomberg Finance LP.

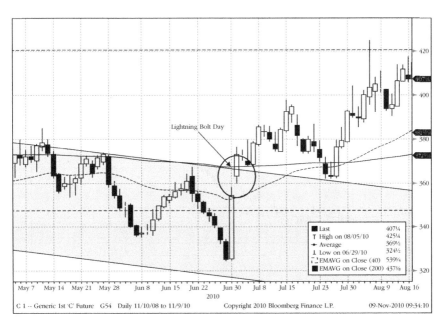

FIGURE 7.22 CBOT Corn Daily, May–August 2010 Hit by Lightning Bolt and Moves Up
Source: Copyright 2010 Bloomberg Finance LP.

FIGURE 7.23 CBOT Oats after Lightning Strike in 2010
Source: Genesis Financial Technologies, Inc.

FIGURE 7.24 AAPL after Lightning Strike in 2003 and into Its Next Peak of 2006
Source: Copyright 2010 Bloomberg Finance LP.

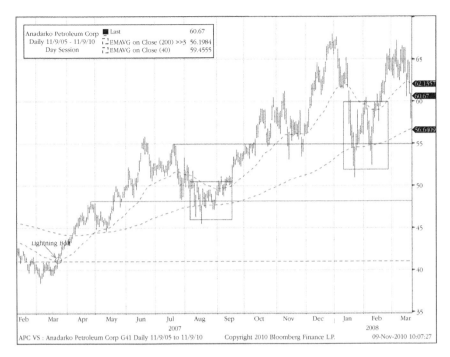

FIGURE 7.25 APC after Lightning Strike in 2007
Source: Copyright 2010 Bloomberg Finance LP.

The approach you take to capture such price moves in Figures 7.23 through 7.28 must match your own tolerance for overall exposure into the bet and potential volatility in both directions. For many traders, *buying into the bolt* is a natural trade and easy to take. For others it is like trying to jump on a moving train when we do not even know where it is headed—a frightening prospect, indeed!

Thinking back to concepts introduced in previous chapters, and without going into great detail, let's briefly review how price unfolded and possible trading strategies for these markets after lightning struck (see Figures 7.29 through 7.32).

Figure 7.29 illustrates that the world had drastically changed for the Oats market after lightning struck on June 9 and 10. A mechanistic trend following—or breakout strategy, where buying is initiated on rules such as a close above the X moving average, or a close above a breakout above the 3-, 5-, or 7-day high—would have you long in this market on June 10, before the confirmation of the lightning bolt strike.

Another method may be to initiate part of a position in anticipation of a possible (and often likely) pullback to the determined breakout range—also known as an *anticipatory strategy* as opposed to a reactive strategy such

FIGURE 7.26 DNR after Lightning Strike in 2007
Source: Copyright 2010 Bloomberg Finance LP.

FIGURE 7.27 AVR after Lightning Strike
Source: Copyright 2010 Bloomberg Finance LP.

FIGURE 7.28 CBOT Corn after Lightning Strike
Source: Copyright 2010 Bloomberg Finance LP.

FIGURE 7.29 Oats
Source: Copyright 2010 Bloomberg Finance LP.

as a breakout buy. Could it be the 2.40 range, or as low as the 2.20–2.25/ bu (dollars per bushel) price range? A method we can use is to determine the key price ranges of previous S&R and the breakout point, and then have sitting buy orders on the potential test down to attempt an entry, or to add to a current long position. I call this the *kiss* entry: This is when price returns to the point of departure before taking off in a particular direction. (We will return to this strategy in Chapter 9.)

As we see in Figure 7.29 on Oats, the market did not return below the lightning bolt pattern, but did have a considerable eight-day pullback to test and find support (price rejection) at the prior price resistance level on June 30.

Of note is that July 2 liquidation of short-term speculative positions is often initiated before going into the U.S. holiday weekend between the 3rd and 4th of that month. This is a common dynamic in the commodity markets before long holidays—often forcing a move counter to the immediate direction of price. We see here market indecision with the narrow price range on July 2 going into the long holiday. On the 5th, when the market opened again, we see buying at the former resistance level, which is now support. This could be a low-risk entry buy with a stop below the new support range of 2.50–2.40.

If you were caught by the surprise of the bolt in Apple (AAPL) like many people were back in 2003, what would have been a strategy to enter the market if you did not want to risk putting all your chips in one basket and jumping onto a running train? You could look to implement some of the same ideas in the review of the Oats charts shown in Figures 7.23 and 7.29: Identify pullback targets of previous support and resistance (acceptance and rejection) ranges. Or, as the market was now a king, and kings return to the valley for regeneration, one could wait for that phase to enter into or add to a position.

Looking carefully at Figure 7.24 of AAPL, the market gave a brief opportunity for entry, or reentry by early June as it probed price at areas of previous resistance. Following the strike, AAPL remained a dominant king into late 2007, when it entered a new two-year cycle down.

Another look at Denbury Resources shows a repeat of the lightning bolt pattern (but just as in nature never exactly the same!). We see a brief opportunity for entry as price returns to the breakup range where the bolt hit. As DNR is now a king (as seen in Figure 7.30), we will watch for (and do see) multiple low-risk opportunities to enter to the long side on this cyclical move. (Please note, we will look at more specific trade entry strategies in Chapter 8.)

In Figures 7.31 and 7.32, we take another look at Avery Dennison (AVY) and the completely unrelated grain commodity, Corn, with the same conceptual focus of entering a market after the bolt strikes.

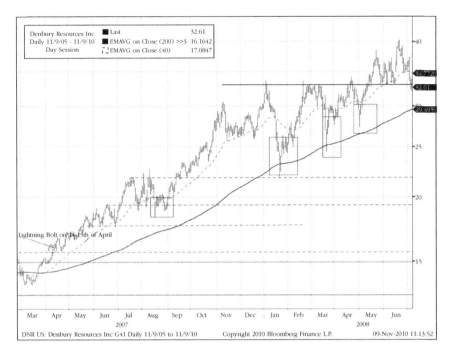

FIGURE 7.30 Entering DNR after Lightning Bolt Strikes
Source: Copyright 2010 Bloomberg Finance LP.

According to our defined pattern rules, AVD was hit by lightning twice in April 2007. If one is not jumping into the market just as lightning strikes, buy orders to enter or add can be placed at the key price range between 24.00 and 25.00 as seen in Figure 7.31. Interestingly, the S&R range of 28.00–30.00, marked the 200-period EMA, where the market launched its decisive next leg to the upside. After breaking up through this resistance range, the market made another test down (to what is now support) in March, May, and June 2010. As of this writing, AVD remains within this range and above new support.

And finally, Figure 7.32 shows the price progression in Corn after a bolt of lightning. With this, we remind ourselves that commodity futures are for the purpose of risk transfer into the future. As it is not possible to actively trade the physical spot market for Corn (which has different pricing depending on delivery terminals, quality, etc.), we look only at the futures contract.

After a bolt hit Corn in the early days of July, we see that the market was up for four to six weeks. Yet, there were only brief low-risk entry opportunities. From July 23 to July 24, the market found support at the breakout and point of lightning bolt strike around 3.76/bu (dollars per bushel).

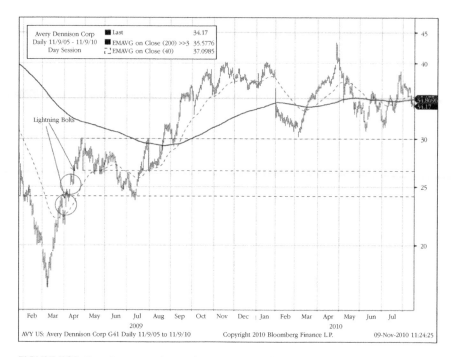

FIGURE 7.31 Entering AVY after Lightning Bolt Strikes
Source: Copyright 2010 Bloomberg Finance LP.

Figure 7.32 depicts this daily price action. Readers may note the strong similarity to the Oats price action.

Conclusion

It is never just one event or condition that builds up to a major storm or memorable market weather or price event. It remains a complex and sensitive system. Our considerations of price patterns defined by familiar conceptual visualizations of the markets may seem at first naïve and simple, but they are helpful when considering any complex systems. As such, describing price conditions with the imagery of complex forces of nature and climate systems makes sense. The markets traders participate in are infinitely complex and thus infinitely sensitive. They are never fully predictable, but with careful observation they are possible to navigate.

Instead of depending on estimations of long-term cycles to predict the unpredictable, it may be better for us to observe only the patterns of price in front of us. With this we can classify the behavior into defined patterns and then determine with a degree of reliability the short-term and overall

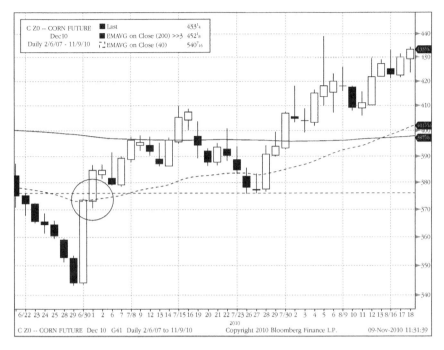

FIGURE 7.32 Entering CBOT Corn after Lightning Bolt Strikes
Source: Copyright 2010 Bloomberg Finance LP.

direction of price after a major pattern event has occurred. The quiet before the storm and the lightning bolt are two price patterns that we can easily scan for and build a trading strategy around.

In this chapter we've covered the appearance of a downward-trend-continuation trigger pattern—the quiet before the storm—and a new-trend-acceleration trigger pattern—the lightning bolt. In the next two chapters covering specific market patterns we try to bring together many of the pattern constellations and concepts into a universal pattern set we call *Adam and Eve*.

CHAPTER 8

Inside Market Cycles

"That means, I think," said Sancho, "that he was exposed to public shame." "That's right," said the convict, "and the crime he was given this punishment for was stockbrokering . . . and also for having a touch of the sorcerer about him."

—*The Ingenious Hidalgo Don Quixote de la Mancha* by Miguel de Cervantes Saavedra. [Translated by John Rutherford, Penguin Books, London (2003), p. 179.]

Polarity, the relationship between two opposites, exists in nature and in markets. The opposites belong to each other and create the whole. We cannot have day without night, joy without despair, or a positive without a negative. As traders and speculators, we act on the understanding and observation that there is indeed cyclical bull and bear behavior in all active markets. The market pendulum swings between the cycle top range to directional trend and cycle bottom range in a complete complex pattern formation in all time frames considered.

Market Entropy

By now readers may recognize that many of the patterns covered in this book are considered with an anticipatory trading approach to identify the ranges of the polar extremes pointing to possible cycle change. To my mind this is only logical. The trader and speculator—the one looking forward—considers a market to anticipate change rather than to react to change after the fact. When we put on a trade, we speculate on a future change in condition; we act to exploit the change or future price event in the market. It is with pattern recognition and visualization methods that anticipatory trading strategies can be developed.

And it is during phases of polar opposites where our risk can be more easily identified. (The idea of risk management with trading pattern recognition methods will be covered in Chapter 9.) For this, the trader's eye can be trained to intuitively see the patterns of a pendulum shift and change. This is where our structured, rule-based thinking meets our developed sense of feeling and intuition. It is the union of our right and left brains working together to complete the whole; it's what gives us the edge. While pattern triggers to a trade are in steady flux and ultimately indiscriminate, developing the natural ability to professionally act on unfolding patterns without the destructive and controlling emotional extremes of fear and greed will be the trader's advantage.

Think about it: The price patterns triggered by disturbances reveal the nature, or condition, of the market. The patterns resulting from human behavior in the marketplace are ultimately driven by universal and repeating human emotions feeding the ongoing cycles. And finally, that polarity is the pivotal element of all cycles.

Against this idea of natural polarity, and that opposites complete the whole, we will look at the elements of pattern constellations exhibited at the start of the pendulum swing of the two cycles—bear bottom and bull top. But first, let's examine the concept of *entropy*.

When thinking about markets, we continue to return to this word. Even with a superficial understanding of entropic systems, the word seems to capture an observed market dynamic. Entropy describes the energy of a certain abstract physical system. The word comes from the Greek *entrope* (change) and is now used to describe, among other things, the increase of potential energy in the universe or any closed system. As you may know from basic physics, most simply, in a cyclical process entropy increases, decreases, and at times remains the same throughout the phases of the cycle. It's sort of like a teakettle. In a teakettle, entropy is the physical dynamic of water molecules constantly seeking equilibrium and stability in spite of periodic disturbances. (This metaphor can then be drawn to price behavior.)

For example, in the morning, you walk into the kitchen and turn on the stove to heat up the water in the kettle. The heat is the trigger and the gradual heat absorption into the water is the disturbance. With the increase in heat, there is a commotion in the water. Before you turned on the heat, the water had been left undisturbed for many hours and was the same temperature as the kettle itself and the surrounding air in your kitchen. The water molecules were free of disturbances all night long and, while entering an increasing state of equilibrium, they became more disordered as you were sleeping. Potential energy (entropic change) was built up overnight. The degree of

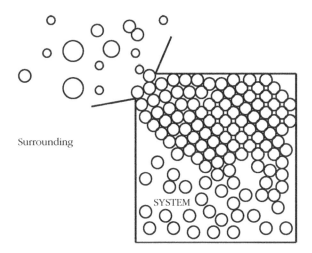

Surrounding

SYSTEM

FIGURE 8.1 Concept of Market Entropy

disorder (or equilibrium in this case) is the degree of entropy and potential energy available for the next cycle. So the greater the entropy (disorder), the greater the potential energy available for directional order (see Figure 8.1).

In this example, heat is the trigger of change for the closed teakettle. So when you shuffled into the kitchen and turned on your stove to heat the disordered water for your morning tea, the heat created a disturbance in the water as it gradually heated up to a boil, creating a high degree of directional order of the water molecules. You then turned off the heat (the agent of change) and the hot water vapor dispersed to the surrounding cold air to again reach equilibrium of temperature. The cycle thus starts again where the water seeks a state of equilibrium. The entropic cycle starts again each day, moving from high entropy with lots of energy potential to low entropy as the energy of the water steams out of the kettle.

Price Cycles

What does entropy have to do with the markets? Markets can be thought of as a closed system, operating in recurring cycles. This model as we understand it can be a parallel concept to the continued struggle in markets as price moves from one polar cycle to the other.

In well over a century of price pattern analysis, there have been detailed descriptions of identifiable patterns at the polar points of cycles. A common one is the graphic head and shoulders to describe price patterns at market tops: a minor price peak (left shoulder) followed by a head peak followed by a second minor price peak (right shoulder). See Figure 8.2.

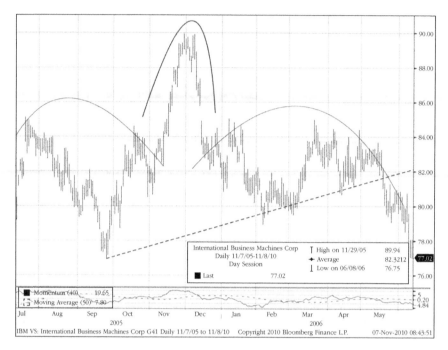

FIGURE 8.2 IBM, Daily. Head and Shoulders
Source: Copyright 2010 Bloomberg Finance LP.

Regardless of the underlying patterns, markets and price behavior can be compared to such closed systems and the thermodynamic behavior inherent to all natural systems. The market moves from a state of disorder with stored-up potential energy (increasing tension), releases the energy as a response to a trigger of change and disturbance, and then seeks equilibrium; the tension, order, and degree of energy build up again for the next cycle of energy release. Each complete cycle and polar extreme shares characteristic price pattern developments and each is triggered by new disturbances in the market.

In this chapter, we examine patterns, such as the *snake* and *Adam and Eve*, that indicate a major cycle shift. With this we also discuss what we will call the *entropic vacuum* (the rapid move to equilibrium), which defines the often-rapid move to the polar bottom or top so the ever-repeating market cycle can continue.

The Snake, the Fake, the Fall, and Adam and Eve

After thinking a lot about the internals of a particular polar top or bottom pattern, calling it Adam and Eve was a natural match for many reasons. I've since discovered that a similar pattern in short-term trading strategies has also been described by Alan S. Farely and also referred to as Adam and Eve.[1] I have taken the liberty of keeping to his nomenclature as the characteristics he describes in the short-term Adam and Eve pattern are, indeed, also seen in many significant market turns. Adam and Eve is the defining component of our pattern for the cyclical bear and bull change.

The Snake Appears, Again

We covered the life of the snake in Chapter 3. Briefly, regardless of the time frame under consideration, when the snake appears, our market is bored. It is in high entropic equilibrium, building energy and waiting for a new reason to act. There are no disturbances and it waits. This is a state of price equilibrium and there is tension (energy) building up for the start of the next cycle. In short, when the snake pattern appears there is high entropy and the hissing sound of accumulating market pressure. As we will see, the snake often appears after a violent and sustained entropic vacuum as the result of a previous polar shift.

The experienced trader and investor resist the tendency to go elsewhere in search of something more active and dynamic, but instead remain attentive to the snake price pattern. Its appearance is critical information because a market in equilibrium has incorporated all information. The price in front of us is stable and oscillating in a narrow range. Yet it is full of energy and potential for rapid change. This potential increases with time as market entropy builds as it waits for new information (a disturbance) to move it out of equilibrium and into the next cycle.

Monitoring this condition is an anticipatory method. Remember, our snake moves back and forth between support and resistance, and can do this for a long time (see Figures 8.3 and 8.4). It does not display a trend. It will lure participants in with false moves. The snake (where the market is building tension) is the bane of trend-following trading approaches because it is full of false breakouts, shallow retracements, and probes below price support; trend-following strategies can be whipped back and forth in and out of a market.

Additionally, there is often moderate volume during this phase because the market signals momentary consensus, agreement, and absorption of all current information and expectations. This is the perfect time for us to anticipate a disturbance, or new information, triggering change in the market.

The Fake

To *fake* or *fake out* is a common expression in sports. The opponents are signaled a pending pass of the ball in one direction, only to have the player

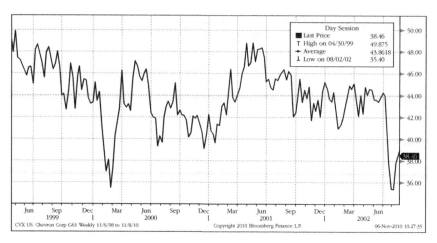

FIGURE 8.3 Snake as Line Chart, Chevron Corp. 1999–2002
Source: Copyright 2010 Bloomberg Finance LP.

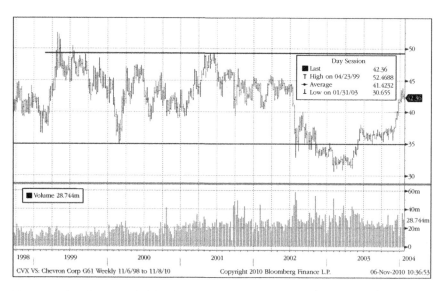

FIGURE 8.4 Snake as Bar Chart with Volume, Chevron Corp. 1999–2003
Source: Copyright 2010 Bloomberg Finance LP.

then fake out his opponents by throwing the ball in the opposite direction. The fake here belongs to the snake of the pattern, also described earlier as the coil of the snake. This is when the market makes what proves to be a *false breakout* in continuation of the preceding trend. This is the last attempt to probe price, bring in the marginal buyers or sellers, increase trade volume, or "fish for stops." It is a test, a deception luring players into

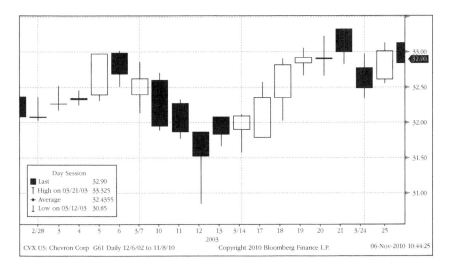

Day Session
■ Last   32.90
T High on 03/21/03 33.325
◆ Average   32.4355
⊥ Low on 03/12/03 30.85

FIGURE 8.5 Chevron Corp., Daily. Detail of the Fake of the Larger Snake Pattern
Source: Copyright 2010 Bloomberg Finance LP.

counterproductive action so they are left holding the bag. And distinguishing the price action of the fake, it is almost *immediately* rejected by the market.

Characteristic of many market cycle bottoms and tops is the fake to the downside or upside before the market moves into its true direction. This is where, for example, at a polar bottom prices spike to new period lows only to find immediate buying with the market rejection of the lower prices.

Of course, this pattern is recognized and confirmed only after the fact. In isolation it tells us little, and (with the exception of short-term trading) it does not meet the criteria of a low-risk trade entry. For us it is a telling directional footprint of a new disturbance in the market, pointing to possible change (again, market entropy).

As we see in Figure 8.5, the snake lures its prey with the fake, or forceful price move in the opposite direction of its real intent. The fake is the moment when the market is tempted to coil into the wrong direction. As we will see, this will be the defining *Adam* element of our cycle bottom pattern. This is the fake, the temptation, and the major trap often seen at market turns.

The characteristic pattern of the fake consists of:

- A price break up or down from a previous price range as determined by most recent price and time S&R levels.
- Often low tick volume.
- Often low trade volume.
- A short time duration: a single in most cases, or very few period bars.

- When viewing intraday price action one may see repeated attempts to probe new highs or lows (depending on the polar cycle) where price is repeatedly rejected.
- A session to close at top, bottom, or midrange of price bar or candle.
- Following price ranges not to exceed the low or high of the fake period move.

This listing has a caveat, though. For short-term traders, this pattern (a new high or low immediately rejected) alone attracts activity. It is a signal to buy or sell the failed move. The fake alone (the period reversal) is not a sign of a major polar cycle change. We will see that it is, however, part of the entire Adam and Eve constellation. The coiled snake with the fake price action wrapped around Adam is the masculine side of the pattern.

Adam

The phase of the pattern we call Adam draws a well-formed reversal in a relatively short time period in the time observed. Like a sword at his side, the fake along with the snake *always* belongs to an Adam phase. He is never without it. It is sharp and decisive. It does not hesitate; the market knows exactly what it wants to do—firmly reject price. In a cycle bottom, Adam slays lower prices without wasting time to turn and make his key move up.

The Adam phase, including the fake, is relatively brief but essential to identifying the polar cyclical pattern. And just as in the biblical parable, Adam succumbs to the temptations initiated by the snake in the garden of the marketplace, and then immediately recognizes his error. The Adam pattern is the first to signal to us the potential consequence of the market action and the impending prevailing direction the market may take.

In summary, the characteristic of Adam is determined immediately after new highs or lows with a decisive price reversal in the opposite direction of the prevailing trend, and within a very short period of time. Adam never appears without the fake first—the pattern that is the market *fall* into temptation. Yet our Adam is decisive, does not vacillate, and knows exactly what he wants to do after the fake of the snake phase lures the market into a strategically wrong move (see Figure 8.6).

Experienced traders will recognize that we are also essentially describing a period of increased price volatility. Volatility in the market can be captured with various sets of measures or indexes. The Adam pattern phase, however, indicates to us the pending appearance of Eve.

When Eve Appears

Hopefully without sounding too clichéd, the *Eve* pattern of course always appears after Adam. Eve never completes or goes beyond the full price range

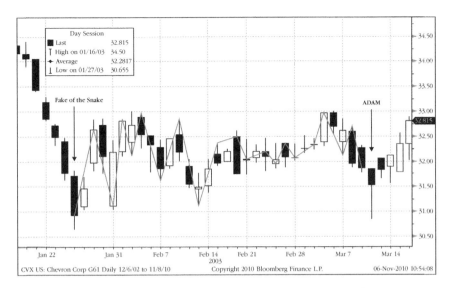

FIGURE 8.6 Adam, Including the Fake, Chevron Corp., January–March 2003, Daily
Source: Copyright 2010 Bloomberg Finance LP.

of Adam. She may shadow or even meet Adam in the test of price, but she never exceeds the Adam phase. (If this were to happen, it would be negated as an Adam and Eve pattern.) The Eve phase may, but must not, retrace the Adam pattern. And in the more complex cycle changes (bottom or top), Adam may appear twice as in the seldom-seen but true double bottom or top pattern. And finally, Adam can often have multiple Eves in his pursuit.

Keep in mind that the emergence of Adam and Eve patterns signals an underlying change in the system. They alert us to something new. Unlike the Adam pattern, which moves quickly, resolutely, and sometimes violently, the Eve phase has a rounded bottom and takes longer (sometimes much longer) to make the decisive move to the upside (or downside in market tops). With the Eve pattern, the market contemplates where, when, and even whether or not it wants to continue.

The appearance of Eve after Adam signals a new and emerging market cycle. Eve is followed by prices ultimately returning to and exceeding the previous support and resistance price range. Her appearance at the edge of a polar end of a cycle confirms the birth of a completely new cycle. This defines the completion of this complex cycle change pattern, as shown in Figure 8.7.

The Falldown or Breakup Stage in the Adam and Eve Pattern

With a *breakup*, the market enters the entropic vacuum phase to the upside, and with the *falldown*, to the downside. It is a decisive part of the Adam and Eve pattern constellation.

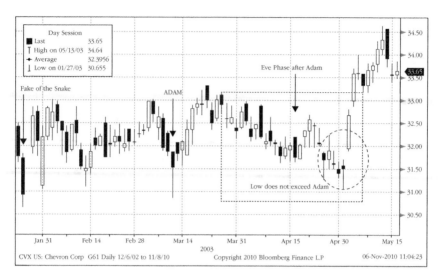

FIGURE 8.7 Appearance of Eve, Chevron Corp., January–May 2003
Source: Copyright 2010 Bloomberg Finance LP.

FIGURE 8.8 Fall of Chevron Corp., 2002
Source: Copyright 2010 Bloomberg Finance LP.

Remaining with the example of Chevron, Figure 8.8 shows that the price entered into an entropic vacuum phase down in the weeks and months before the Adam and Eve phase could develop in late 2002 and early 2003 (as seen in Figure 8.6). Here we see that price searches for a new

FIGURE 8.9 The Fall: American Apparel Inc., October 2007–October 2008 with retracement "kiss."
Source: Copyright 2010 Bloomberg Finance LP.

state of equilibrium so the cycle of polarity can start once again after the falldown of mid 2002.

Characteristics of the *falldown* or *breakup* phase that ultimately leads to Adam, Even, and a new entropic phase of the complete pattern include:

- At the time of breakup or falldown, price movement is around the lower (or higher in the case of the breakup) band of S&R, and often on high volume.
- In a falldown, price often shows short-term support at a lower price band before the final selloff. (This is sometimes recognized as the right shoulder of a head-and-shoulders pattern.)
- In a breakup, price often shows short-term resistance at the upper price band before the final burst of buying to initiate the breakup.
- At the time of breakup or falldown, price closes at or near a period low or high (depending on the cycle direction) in the period price bar.
- If there is retracement to (or a return to kiss as demonstrated in Figure 8.9) the breakup or falldown price range (often clearly previous support or resistance) it is immediately met with price rejection at what is now new resistance or support. This retracement phase of the pattern is the Eve period.
- Following completion of Eve (and confirmation of the polar cycle bottom or top), there is an extended and rapid trend move from the break line as the market enters the new entropic vacuum stage before the cycle begins again.

The breakup or falldown is often the ultimate price response to any new disturbance (i.e., new information) in the market. For Chevron, we observed a breaking apart of equilibrium with the emergence of the Adam and Eve pattern, which was our initial commotion in the marketplace where new information was coming into the market and price was responding (as water responds to the trigger of heat). As we see in Figure 8.10, price later rapidly broke *up*. The market entropy vacuum, phase is where price must do the natural work of probing for a price level in search of new equilibrium. It can be to the up- or the downside. As this unfolds, price will often overextend itself to a new range of price and its ultimate rejection range as the cycle starts again (Figure 8.10).

Practical Examples

Earlier, we briefly mentioned and described the well-known *head-and-shoulders* pattern. Readers may recognize characteristics of the head-and-shoulders pattern in our demonstrations of the Adam and Eve complex pattern, in particular, the head and right shoulder pattern segments. Our purpose now is to go between the lines and inside this pattern (into the *granularity* of this broadly descriptive pattern).

Let's look at both past and relatively current examples of Northrop Grumman Corp. (NOC), a global provider of manufacturing and services to the aerospace, electronics, and shipbuilding industries (Figure 8.11).

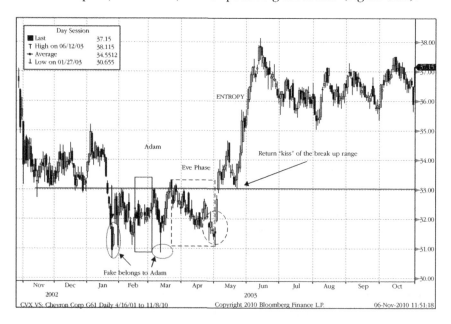

FIGURE 8.10 Chevron Corp. after Completion of Adam and Eve Pattern Cycle
Source: Copyright 2010 Bloomberg Finance LP.

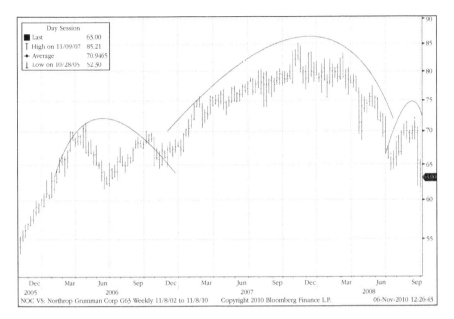

FIGURE 8.11 NOC: Classic Head-and-Shoulders Pattern
Source: Copyright 2010 Bloomberg Finance LP.

Figures 8.12 and 8.13 illustrate from the lows of 2003 that NOC was still in a secular long-term uptrend that continued into 2007. In the fall of 2007, the market enters a snake phase as price oscillates between 75 and 80. Then in October 2007 we have the fake to new highs of 85.00 only to be met with an almost immediate rejection of higher prices (Figure 8.13).

The snake had wrapped itself around Adam in this topping pattern. Then, true to the behavior of the Eve phase of our polar cycle pattern, Eve emerges and follows Adam. Price never exceeds the fake and the Adam price stage; Eve is a long phase where the market meanders for a period of four months as it attempts to decide direction.

Figure 8.14 shows that on April 14, the market finally makes its move out of the complete snake pattern, including the Adam and Eve phases within it. And, as is often seen with the first falldown (reviewed earlier in this chapter), the market returns to the fall line (or previous support). This return to previous support, sometimes with multiple attempts, is also the phase of the pattern that creates the beginning of what is commonly described as the right shoulder of the large head-and-shoulders formation (see Figure 8.11).

For Northrop Grumman, the fall appears on September 17 as it enters into its entropic vacuum phase to find new equilibrium and garner energy (Figure 8.14).

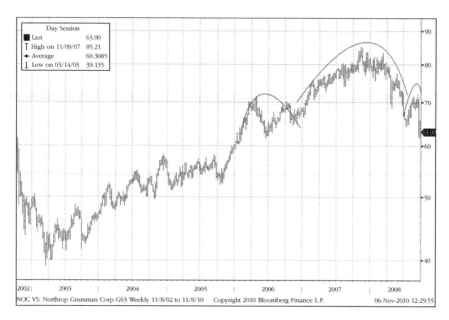

FIGURE 8.12 NOC from Lows of 2003
Source: Copyright 2010 Bloomberg Finance LP.

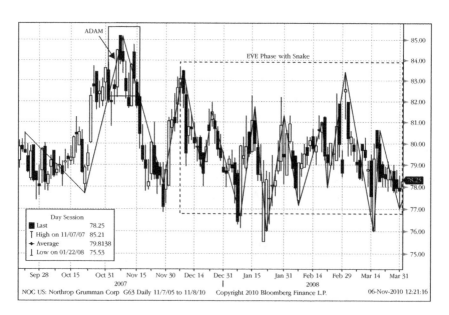

FIGURE 8.13 NOC in Snake/Adam/Eve Pattern Phase, 2007–2008
Source: Copyright 2010 Bloomberg Finance LP.

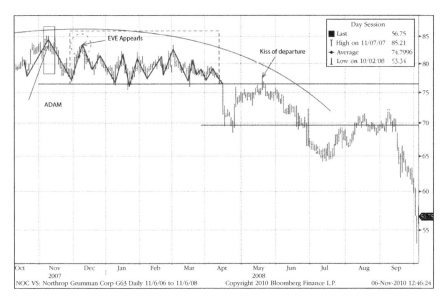

FIGURE 8.14 Fall of Northrop Grumman with Adam/Eve/Snake Pattern Top Phase
Source: Copyright 2010 Bloomberg Finance LP.

The Breakup in Market Bottoms

For some reason inherent in human nature, most of us are interested in a market poised to go the upside. On this note, we examined the recent cycle pattern in a polar bottom of an oil exploration and production company, Chevron Corporation, and now look more closely at the oil field service provider, Schlumberger, Ltd.

Unlike a firm such as American Apparel, which remains in a downward spiral after its break (as seen in Figure 8.9), these firms belong to the cyclical energy industry. After the severe cyclical downturns through the 1990s, they entered into a relatively long period of price equilibrium (characterized by high entropy and degree of potential energy) before prices bottomed in 2002–2003, and took off to the upside into multiyear secular cycles with highs for Schlumberger Ltd. into 2007 and 2008—when a new cycle down into 2009 emerged (see Figure 8.15).

Figures 8.15a, 8.15b, and 8.15c depict a daily, weekly, and monthly chart as the cycle bottom unfolded. What were the patterns within the complex, alerting us to the start of a new cycle?

A view of the weekly chart of SLB (see Figure 8.15a) shows our previously described snake appearing after the fall in August. Here it entered the entropic vacuum on its way searching for equilibrium.

In Figure 8.15c, the chart is simpler. We see that between December and March, the market made multiple attempts to go lower. This was the

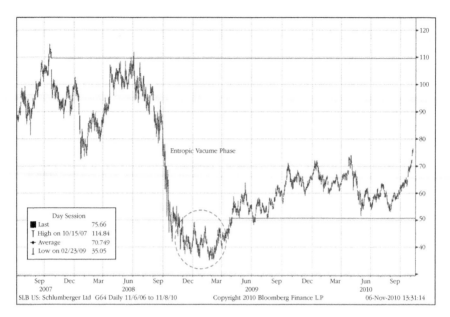

FIGURE 8.15 Fall of Schlumberger Ltd.: Entropic Vacuum, Entropy Phase, and Break to the Upside of New Cycle, Spring 2009
Source: Copyright 2010 Bloomberg Finance LP.

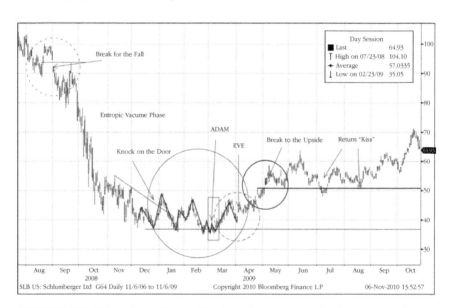

FIGURE 8.15A SLB, Daily, with Identification of a Knock on the Door, the Snake, and Adam and Eve
Source: Copyright 2010 Bloomberg Finance LP.

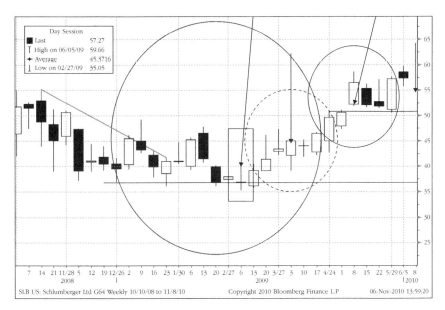

FIGURE 8.15B SLB, Weekly, Where Adam Period Is Identified as Key Reversal Bottom (Breakup in May Clearly Identified by Weekly Chart)
Source: Copyright 2010 Bloomberg Finance LP.

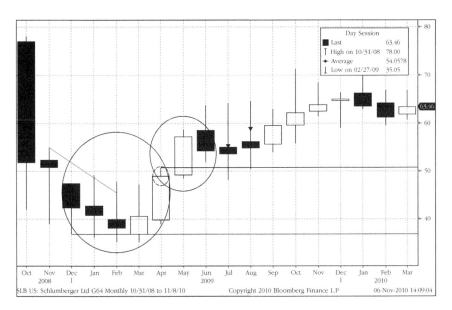

FIGURE 8.15C SLB, Monthly
Source: Copyright 2010 Bloomberg Finance LP.

period of the snake. In March we had what is recognized as a bullish engulfing pattern candlestick over February, which is quite a bullish signal considering not only the time period of the candle pattern (monthly), but the daily and weekly price action within this monthly pattern.

When Wheat Turns

While commodity markets are not capitalization markets, these also attract more interest when they are headed to the upside, even though trading and profit opportunities in commodity markets are absolutely independent of market direction. Among the most cyclical commodity markets are the renewable grain markets, and within the grain complex, wheat is grown throughout the world in spring and winter. It is second only to rice as the most-consumed grain in the world. This fundamental fact alone contributes to relatively stable prices for Wheat over time, and explains why trend cycles are short.

Grains are, after all, renewable foods. They grow. While producing only 10 percent of the world's wheat, the United States is the largest exporter. There are three classes of wheat actively traded on the U.S. exchanges: Soft Red Winter Wheat (Chicago Board of Trade), Hard Red Winter Wheat (Kansas City Board of Trade), and Hard Red Spring Wheat (Minneapolis Board of Trade). All classes of Wheat contracts are important for the commercial hedger. The largest volume of Wheat contracts traded, however, is the Winter Wheat contract traded at the Chicago Board of Trade. For this reason, we will take a look at the Chicago Wheat in Figure 8.16.

The great Wheat bull market of 2008 is still fresh in many of our minds. As we see in Figure 8.16, Wheat had what can now be termed a mini-rally in late 2006 (a foreshadowing and knock on the door of a larger bull market on the way?). Looking more closely at this cycle in the figure, we can now easily identify our snake, including Adam (with the fake), Eve (with the decision-making and price testing), and the definitive break to the upside in 2007.

Let's look at the details of the price action at this cycle bottom before Wheat exploded to the upside in the bull market of 2008 (see Figures 8.17 and 8.18).

Please note the classic temptation within the Adam phase of this cycle bottom. It appears as a fake over two days to stop and completely recover and exceed the prior price range. The price action tells of immediate rejection of lower price and market recognition of an error—a mispricing.

Then into May and early June—in the Eve phase of the pattern following Adam—the market retraces to test lower prices at the previously established support ranges. Over the next two weeks, in completion of the Eve phase, prices inch up higher. On June 11, 2007—after the complex

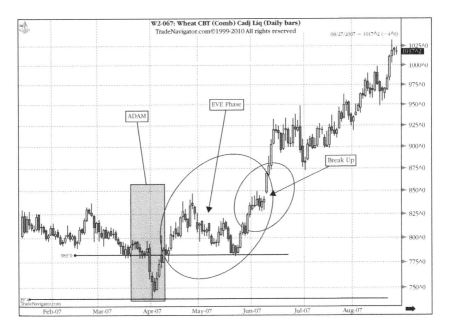

FIGURE 8.16 CBOT Wheat, Vacuum to the Upside
Source: Genesis Financial Technologies, Inc.

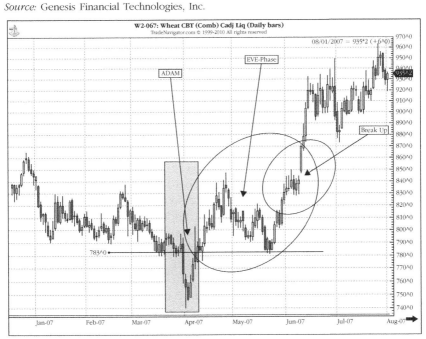

FIGURE 8.17 CBOT Wheat, Spring 2007, Daily. Detail Pattern of Cycle Bottom
Source: Genesis Financial Technologies, Inc.

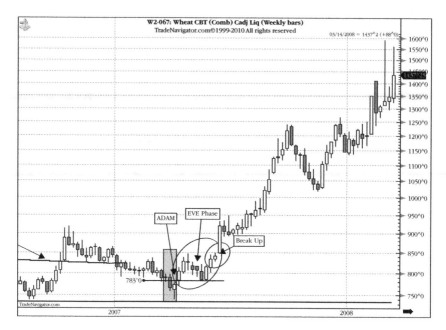

FIGURE 8.18 CBOT Wheat, Weekly. Following the Birth and Breakout
Source: Genesis Financial Technologies, Inc.

Adam/Eve pattern—lightning strikes the Wheat market. Price opens above the high of the previous session and exceeds all resistance levels of the past year. A new market phase is born. (See Figure 8.19.)

More recently, after an extended down-cycle phase from the highs in 2008, we entered into yet another up-cycle phase. This polar bottom was also marked by the appearance of the snake with the Adam and Eve pattern bottom (see Figures 8.20 and 8.21).

Into the spring of 2010, we see in Figures 8.20 and 8.21 what appears to be the last leg of the severe cycle down from the highs of 2008. This same period is shown with two separate sources, to illustrate that when we attempt to position ourselves into a trade against a larger unfolding pattern that may take days and weeks to confirm itself, we cannot put too much weight on exact S&R levels in the micro-view. For example, support breakdown in what proved to be a fake was at 505.1/4 in Figure 8.20 and 507.3/4 in Figure 8.21.

The Adam phase of this polar bottom cycle was put in between June 6 and 9. The pattern within the cycle is quite similar to the earlier cycle bottom of March 2007. (See Figures 8.16 and 8.17—at that time, the Eve phase of the pattern was relatively short and made only a brief probe to test lower prices.)

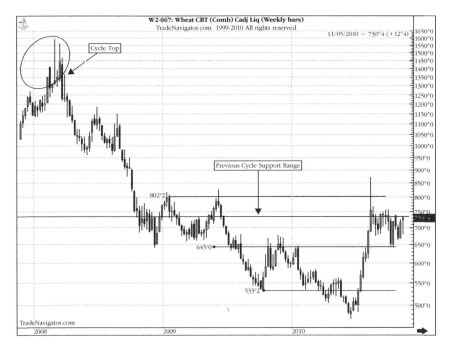

FIGURE 8.19 CBOT Wheat. Two-Year Weekly of Cycle Top and Entropic Vacuum Selloff to New Polar Cycle

Note price action at cycle top in the weeks of February and March 2008 where price paid by last marginal buyers was immediately rejected by the market.

Source: Genesis Financial Technologies, Inc.

As seen in Figures 8.20 and 8.21, price recovered to the prior support range and made the characteristic test retracement to probe market acceptance of lower prices. Following the down day of June 29, price was immediately and convincingly rejected on June 30 and even exceeded previous price resistance. The price action of July 2 is reminiscent of the lightning bolt pattern, signaling new information and major change.

Resulting from this most recent polar bottom pattern is the entropic vacuum phase where price rapidly marches to the next equilibrium phase where conditions for the next directional order of price are built up (see Figure 8.22).

Summary

When using pattern recognition, before allocating capital to a trade we have to define the market structure. The above discussion is one of many price and pattern structures indicating a direction. If you go back through

FIGURE 8.20 CBOT Wheat. Detail of Daily Bottoming Pattern, June–July 2010
Source: Genesis Financial Technologies, Inc.

FIGURE 8.21 CBOT Wheat Detail of Daily Bottoming Pattern
Source: Copyright 2010 Bloomberg Finance LP.

FIGURE 8.22 CBOT Wheat, Daily. New Adam and Eve Cycle Bottom and Entropic Vacuum Move Up

Source: Genesis Financial Technologies, Inc.

the price action of Chicago Wheat, for example, there were a few periods that could have developed into an Adam and Eve bottom—the bottoming action of September–October 2009 as an example. The price deterioration and weakening in January and February invalidated the action of early October as an Adam and Eve bottom. (See Figure 8.20.) The pattern can be confirmed only with a clearly definitive breakup (or falldown as the case may be) from the Eve range where price is testing to get an answer from the collective market for definitive direction.

With proper trade management, the pattern can be used for timing to position oneself in the direction and commit to the trade with confirmation.

Conclusion

The ideas of polarity of cycles with identified and named patterns from the lightning bolt to the Valley of the Kings to Adam and Eve aid us in conceptualizing market visualization. In this chapter, we covered what I call a *universal pattern constellation* of ongoing change that includes the pattern elements of entropy, the snake, the fake, the falldown or breakup, and Adam and Eve. It is a conceptual visualization of ongoing change in the markets and its associated patterns. With a vision we have a plan, and with a plan we know what to do. And knowing what to do is the critical factor in good risk management.

To bring this together for action and sound trading strategies, however, we must apply specific trading tactics with risk management to our pattern analysis. Without a handle on the big subject of risk in trading, no matter how terrific our analysis and trade timing, our efforts may still produce poor or even disastrous returns. It is said—and I believe this—that with great risk management, even the most mediocre trading strategy can produce positive returns over time. Controlling risk is at least half (maybe even more) of the equation for success. For some reason, though, we pay less attention to considering risks than "calling the market," perhaps because risk management is the dull side of the trade. Knowing and acting on sound rules of risk management does not grab attention and create the excitement of a great market call.

Risk consideration is a major subject. It includes understanding position size management, use of leverage, understanding risk factors inherent in markets traded, condition of markets traded (volatility, liquidity, etc.), and even personal and operational risk. In Chapter 9 we will consider risk and trade management in the context of specific trades taken.

CHAPTER 9

Managing Risk with Applied Trading Tactics

"O lady of my soul, Dulcinea, flower of all beauty, succor this your knight who, through his desire to satisfy your great goodness, finds himself in this dire peril!" Uttering these words, gripping his sword, raising his shield and launching himself at the Basque was the work of a moment, as Don Quixote resolved to venture everything on the fortune of a single blow.
—The Ingenious Hidalgo Don Quixote de la Mancha by Miguel de Cervantes Saavedra. [Translated by John Rutherford, Penguin Books, London (2003), p. 70.]

Risk management might be the Holy Grail for any trading strategy. As most experienced traders and money managers agree, good risk management can make even the most mediocre trading methods successful, and will immensely enhance good methods. In spite of this, it may be the most neglected factor of successful trade management. We have libraries of books, tapes, and videos on trade entry setups and price forecasting methods and rules that do not even touch on risk considerations for trading. And even when they do, it may be only in passing. It can be like getting lessons on how to ride a bike, but without learning about the brakes. How is it that risk—a topic so critical to the success of any trading strategy—could be so woefully neglected in the literature in the field?

The answer may be found in the same reason many politicians and government officials neglect infrastructure development for transportation, water, energy, and sewage lines. While critical to our well-being, it is invisible; it is not exciting and it does not provide us the immediate satisfaction of building, let's say, a sports stadium or the new "tallest" skyscraper.

We do not *see* risk and money management. It cannot be easily explained in a sound bite. But like a market called right with a trade timed and executed to the perfection of an atomic clock, without the unseen infrastructure of managing risks and money, it can be for naught and turn into the trade from hell just as that stadium or skyscraper could decay away to an expensive, empty windblown shell.

To Play and Make Merry

In trading, when thinking about risk we cannot forget that there is a difference between speculation and gambling. *Gambling* comes from the old German word *gamen* (or *gameln*), to play and make merry, which leads to the modern German word, *vergameln*—ruined, rotted, or wasted. On the other hand, the Latin *speculari*—to view, observe, watch, and ponder—is the root of *speculation*. The gambler is the game player who seeks an edge through very large numbers. The speculator is the one who waits, watches, and observes. I hold the idea that the road to success and risk management is not only trading based on a numbers game (often a numerical model built from a system unrelated to what we are trading); and that trading based *only* on the rules of gaming will lead to ruin.

Measuring the Future

The future will always be unknown. In any transaction, we are dealing with change, which brings risk. We accept it as a part of our business. When we bank on change, more often than not, events will not unfold just as we anticipate and *hope*. Risk is always ahead of us. It is always unknown and not in the events of the past. Yet, somehow, we continue to build risk metrics and models (often using gaming models) on the measured events of the past, with little thought to the future. And when putting on a trade that will have a future outcome, we most often base our thinking *only* on past data (i.e., the basis of the LTCM model discussed in Chapter 1) without imagining the future with, for example, scenario building.

In his book, *Beyond Fear and Greed,* Hersh Shefrin makes a fair and valid criticism: "Technical analysts are prone to making excessively volatile predictions because they are like generals who continually fight the last war."[1] (One might make the same criticism of bankers who use the oft-inane "credit score" models in lieu of knowing their customer, but that is another topic.) When we are thinking about managing a trade and the risk associated with a trade, perhaps we can move away from acting like the general fighting that last long-ago war, and instead build our actions on the ever-changing facts on the ground, including scenario building.

One thing we know for sure: As change unfolds, bad things happen. Disastrous losses in market lore (some covered here in this book) and even the significant trading loss I incurred (which I will share later in this chapter) happen because there was a scenario, an outcome, that was never considered, or worse, not even understood as a possibility.

In sum, when we enter a transaction, we accept a risk to try to realize a reward. Managing risk is identifying the risk as much as possible, determining what acceptable risk is, and creating risk action scenarios. The most basic considerations before we enter any trade include: How can we lose, and how much are we willing to lose to stay in the game?

Metrics of Risk

Metrics of risk is a very large and important subject in finance; we can take from the playbook of fund and portfolio management and apply some of the ideas of risk measurement tools to our own work. These tools will never reduce risk in itself, but they can help us understand our overall performance and the quantified risk we take to achieve it. This is not intended to be an exhaustive review of the portfolio manager's toolbox to measure risk, but a brief review to help us think about our own trading risk.

Value at Risk

Definitions of *value at risk (VaR)* will be slightly different depending on the source. But all essentially define VaR as a risk measure of "the predicted worst-case loss." These metrics are relatively new (coming into greater use after the 1987 crash) and many make assumptions based on normal market conditions and past data. Before briefly covering risk valuation metrics, there is a caveat.

Reliance on standard risk valuations can cause us to take our eye off the market and the nature of our portfolio (or trading account) and indulge the tendency to measure only the risk, but not the *how* and *why* we make the decisions for a trade. In other words, relying on external standards can reduce us to not knowing what we are doing. And this is a possible disconnect. For example, based on metrics alone of a potential loss (due to volatility, contract sizing, etc.), we can construe an equal VaR metric for a contract for Palladium and for the S&P E-mini-contract. But the Palladium contract may be inherently much more risky due to considerations such as liquidity. An accepted VaR metric may never capture this.

Drawdown: Losing versus Gaining—What Does It Cost You?

A *drawdown* measures the decline in Net Asset Value (NAV) from a historic high point; and considers the length (in time) and depth of a losing period during an investment holding period. Tracking this, just as a professional tracks his performance, gives us information on the truth behind our performance. This is easily measured and defined as the percent retrenchment from a performance peak to a valley low. Monitoring drawdowns also encompasses time as it measures a drawdown of a period from equity peak to equity valley (*length of drawdown*) and the time from the equity valley to a new equity high (*time to recovery*). This tells how long it has taken us to recover from losses. Ask yourself: Is it acceptable to have a drawdown of 50 percent over 12 months for a 5 percent return? Depending on what you trade, your strategy, and account size, you might think it is. But if you regularly have a drawdown of that magnitude, the chances of longer-term survival are practically zero.

How about the amount you need to earn to return to a high-water mark (previous equity high) after a losing streak? This metric (losing streak) is the percentage change between the equity high (your high-water mark) and the latest month's or period equity. This statistic tells us the percentage you need to overcome in order to exceed a high-water mark and be profitable again from the starting period.

Gain-to-Loss Ratio

This is a simple ratio of the average gain in a gaining period divided by the average loss in a losing period. Periods can be monthly or quarterly depending on the time frame you want to consider. It can alert us to the dreadful tendency for many traders to accept a running series of small gains, only to lose with a few large losses.

Profit-to-Loss Ratio

This combines the gain-to-loss ratio and the ratio of the percentage of profitable periods or trades to the percentage of losing periods or trades—in other words, the historical ability for your system or method to generate profits over losses. Since the profit-to-loss ratio considers both the average size and the frequency of winning and losing, it also gives us a history of the ratio of dollars earned in the investment over dollars lost. For example, a profit-to-loss ratio of 2.00 means that, historically, the investment earned 2.00 of profit for each 1.00 of risk (or loss) taken, or 2:1—a historically profitable method. However, this metric tells us nothing about other risks taken to achieve the gain. For this, many will consider volatility measurements of the position while holding. We will cover volatility shortly.

The Standard Deviation on Return

Standard deviation on return is a measurement of what statisticians call the *dispersal* or uncertainty in a random variable. In our case the random variable is your return on investment. Standard deviation will tell us the degree of variation of returns around the average return. The higher the volatility of your returns, the greater the standard deviation. For this reason, the standard deviation is often used as a measure of investment risk.

The Sharpe Ratio

Many of us are familiar with the *Sharpe ratio* (developed by economist William Sharpe). This still-popular *risk-adjusted* return measure attempts to tell us the ongoing risk taken for performance return achieved. "Risk adjusted" is the key measure here, indicating how much theoretical risk we take to achieve a return.

The *return* is defined as the average return of an investment over the risk-free rate. The *risk-free rate* is generally the return on something like three-month Treasury bills. *Risk* is defined as the standard deviation or volatility (see above) of the investment returns. The more return data points we have (usually measured monthly), the more significant these metrics are in telling us how much risk we took to achieve our returns. The higher your Sharpe ratio, the better the returns relative to the amount of risk taken.

SORTINO RATIO An additional metric that is similar to the Sharpe ratio, but tells us more about the possible risk taken to achieve performance, is the *Sortino ratio*. This uses the *downside deviation* instead of the standard deviation, which does not single out and capture up or down volatility included in any performance. For this reason, many analysts considering downside risk prefer to measure the Sortino ratio.

The Micro-View of Risk: How Much Can You Lose on Your Trade?

Some might argue that position sizing is money management and not risk management. I hold that any considerations and actions taken to assure ongoing financial health around a transaction belong under the umbrella of risk management and this discussion. What, then, is the total size of your position relative to your portfolio or cash and what downside impact can it have on your total account? Working out your position sizing based on cash required to hold it (i.e., how much margin must be held in your account) tells us how much of your account may be risked for position.

A trading system or method might tell us to go long or short, but only you can determine how *much* or the *size* of the trade. There are numerous philosophies and approaches to this, mostly based on rules of gaming. One example of a method is for the trader to set a fixed percentage of equity or margin based on changes in capital. Another is to take a strict position sizing method independent of the account size—to always enter the position with the same number of lots. The higher the fixed percentage used relative to capital in your account, the more aggressive the trading method.

This method does not allow the account to grow in geometrical progression and does not consider the market condition. When considering these position-sizing methods, the market reality is that flexibility must be maintained. In leveraged markets such as futures on commodities, a "small" position can suddenly require much more margin than it did 24 hours ago due to changes in price volatility, and so on.

Money Management

Ralph Vince has done much work on trade sizing and money management and is best known for the *optimal f* (optimal fixed fraction) system[2] to determine the ideal fraction of your money to allocate per trade for the highest performance and based on past performance. (He recently expanded this work in his book[3], *The Leverage Space Trading Model*.) The logic of the strategies and testing them on your own portfolio can be a real eye-opener to the power of leveraging for both enormous gains and rapid ruin.

Interestingly, Vince's work on optimal *f* was to improve on the *Kelly f*, a concept that came from a Bell Labs researcher. This researcher, John Kelly, observed that there was an analogy between growth rate of a trading account and the rate of information transmission packets through a communications channel, such as a telephone line. This led to the Kelly formula, which was a predetermined optimal bet size. It assumed that the losses and wins will stay the same (not too different from information transmission packets in a controlled setting).

These are insightful methods, but they may have shortcomings in the real world. For example, a series of losing trades can be substantially higher than a single loss, or the external risk influences are not even considered. In spite of this, one can adopt many of the concepts in money management and modify them to one's situation and comfort level. The work of

Vince and others is essential to constructing risk-management methods for successful trading.

Risk and Time

Every trade has a life cycle imposed either by the trader or by the market. Either way, time is a risk factor. And from the time you enter a trade to the time you close a trade, stuff will happen. The longer the time horizon, the more likely unforeseen influences will play into price. We usually accept this, and sometimes, such as with day trading strategies, we must limit the life of a trade. (Before the advent of low costs in executing and electronic trading platforms for the general public, short-term trading was limited to the professional arena.)

When we trade, how do we factor in time and risk? For example, a trader might buy a stock index with positive return expectation over a times scale of X. After the return expectation does not materialize, do you close the position just because the time factor of your risk-management rules says to get out now? Some would say "yes," as your risk has theoretically increased. Others might say to "just put in a stop-loss order, forget about it, and go play golf."

My answer touches on *scenario building* (discussed in this chapter) and the need for constant reevaluation of a trade. That is how I deal with time. Once a trade is on, instead of being a slave to a rule (as with anything in life), know when to ditch the rule when it does not apply to the real-world situation. With the risk of time, the position must be critically and regularly reevaluated. Ask yourself whether the initial reason for the trade is still valid. Or has there been a change where you can no longer justify holding the position? Or maybe some new information has come to you and you reasonably anticipate that significant news may hit the market tomorrow, positively affecting your position. Would you close out the trade just because your timeline and expectation rule demand it?

There may be other occasions when the risk of time is imposed on the decision whether or how to trade.

TIME AS A TRADER-IMPOSED RISK An *imposed risk* is independent of the market and instrument traded. For example, when considering time the possibility of losing significantly on an investment presents much more risk for an older investor entering retirement than for the younger investor, regardless of the potential reward. The trade is the same, but there is more risk for the older investing group than for the younger. The retiree simply does not have the time and opportunity potential for recovery after a loss; the younger investor, with time on his or her side, has an overall reduced risk of the trade. The same can be said on the more micro-level of the trade where we have funds available for a limited time. The trade is inherently more risky due to the externally imposed risk of time limitations.

As an aside: One of the beauties of using point and figure charts is that they do not scale according to time—making any volatility measurement a constant and removing the consideration of a predetermined lifetime of a position.

VOLATILITY IN TIME: WHAT HAPPENS BETWEEN ENTRY AND EXIT
Most trading strategies concern entry and exit but not what happens in between (the volatility), which is also a cost to the position and to your portfolio and therefore a factor of risk.

We've touched on this concerning an overall portfolio. Overall market volatility is a decisive factor and is why we have, for example, the CBOE VIX future to actually hedge the risk of volatility of the overall stock market. Volatility is measured, hedged, and also traded (i.e., in options strategies where volatility is factored into the price, where higher volatility of the underlying increases the price of the option).

Depending on the market condition, the value of any position will vary from day to day, and even hour to hour. The amount of change measured in degree and time is price volatility, and is considered by most not to be a good thing. This is because price fluctuation associated with high volatility in both directions causes concern and increased uncertainty. It introduces doubt.

This may sound like circular logic, but ultimately we cannot precisely measure risk in volatility because volatility itself is volatile and does not occur in regular sequence (like telephone-line data packets). At the same time, a market void of volatility is not necessarily one that is void of risk. Volatility itself is not risk. At its relatively lowest point, volatility may even present high risk. Think about the snake phase of a market, or the illustration of entropy going from an ordered state into rapid disorder in Chapter 8. What may seem like an orderly, low-risk state could be everything but.

Finally, the subject of market volatility is extensive and beyond the purpose of this book. *The overall point is that volatility must be considered an internal risk of the market.* And this risk can impose a behavior risk on a trader that affects his or her ability for position management. Volatility is therefore a forward dimension of price and of risk, and it comes with a cost. Before entering a trade, ask yourself whether you are prepared for the expected cost of volatility to your account as well as the potential emotional demand.

Scenario Building: Before the Trade

Betting everything on a single outcome is effectively gambling that the outcome you desire will be what happens. ("There is a 90% probability!")

We're interested in speculation, regardless of the ill-deserved modern negative associations with the word. For each trade, sound risk management requires that we first consider as many events as we can possibly imagine as well as what we need to do in the event of loss and unforeseen conditions.

War games (mock wartime battles) and simulations are an arena where ongoing scenario building is an essential part of battle training. It is the staple of the planning model to work through as many scenarios and external influences onto the outcome as possible. With each imagined scenario is a planned and rehearsed action. Often by simply exploring risk scenarios, new and unknown risk potentials are discovered. Of course, for trading, we do not need the elaborate models of war games, but the premise is the same and we can incorporate it into our work and risk management routine.

If this sounds so obviously logical, why is it that even the most sophisticated institutions often project a single outcome—that the transaction will be successful—and then act? Forecasting appeals to our needs for certainty. Business decisions are built and executed upon forecasts and rarely on scenarios. Resources are allocated, for example, according to sales forecasts.

We see the power and influence of forecasting every day. This morning a major financial network was interviewing a currency analyst and her final question was, "Where do you think the dollar will be headed in the next few months?" This analyst gave not only the direction, but even an absolute target. This is *not* good information, but rather morning chatter. The trader does not need to be certain of a direction and target, but does need to be certain of what actions to take upon market eventualities.

When entering a trade, do not forecast. Develop scenarios, starting with the worst-case scenario. That will give us our real VaR.

Applying Trading Tactics in Your Scenario

Making money by trading is done by recognizing and acting on the opportunities the markets present to us. We've presented a few methods of pattern recognition to detect change and opportunity. Some would say it is nothing more than this. If this were so, how is it that our oil trader in Chapter 4 who recognized and acted on the opportunities in the 2008 Crude Oil market could blow out so spectacularly when he not only called it right, but acted on his call? If you have read thus far, you have seen that our trader lost at the onset regardless of calling it right. What was ignored? Time, volatility, position size relative to cash at hand, external operational risk when putting partners in his operation (his FCM) at unqualified risk, no obvious plan (otherwise the account would have been properly funded), and possibly all the risks associated with hubris and greed when going for the big hit. Any single factor alone could sink a trade no matter how great the call. It's similar to chess; he lost in the very first moves regardless of how well he played.

Do Your Homework

In 1997, Nassim Taleb wrote what was then a very profound essay to refute the increasingly popular value-at-risk (VaR) model. After reading it, I was moved to immediately write him and a day later he graciously wrote back acknowledging the appreciation of his then-little-known work. This essay can still be found in its entirety[4] and remains a timeless list of risk rules. The first rule was: "Do not venture in markets and products you do not understand. You will be a sitting duck." And the last rule, number nine, was, "Read every book by traders to study where they lost money. You will learn nothing relevant from their profits (the markets adjust). You will learn from their losses."

Rule number one goes back to universal wisdom. Do your homework. Understand the details of the instrument you will trade (delivery date, front month expiry and trading rules, commercial to speculative participation, point size, exit rules, who is the counterparty, exchange rules). Telling your broker or exchange that you "didn't know" the front month had no trading limits as the market went threefold beyond what you *thought* was a price limit does not get you out of a margin requirement or the bad trade and is no different from saying "my dog ate it" in primary school. In other words, if you do not know the rules, and therefore you cannot know what to do next you may be at the highest level of risk—the seconds before the deer-caught-in-the-headlights state.

Operational Risk: Who Are All These Players and What Risk Do They Bring?

Operational risk is defined by the Basel II Accord as "the risk of loss resulting from inadequate or failed internal processes, people and systems or external events."[5] This is broadly defined as a guideline for institutions, but we can take this definition for our own understanding of operational risk.

While it is often said that trading in active markets is a lonely endeavor—and on one level this is indeed the case—we cannot trade without a market, service providers, and a community of participants. Think about the actors in this endeavor: your broker, the analysts who send e-mails to you, the advisors, the exchanges, the commercial traders, the system vendors, software packages, data vendors, and the background chorus also known as "other traders"—people like you and me—the floor traders, the specialists, the funds, the hedgers. How can you make sure that these players are not a distraction increasing your risk? Evaluate each one carefully and if you find that individual X or Service Y is an attention stealer or an ongoing distraction, he or she is also a risk factor.

We've all heard the reasons: "My data connection was down"; "The order-entry platform did not work"; "I was traveling and did not have a good Internet connection"; "I could not reach the trading floor." These operational risks can also be avoided with scenario building.

Your Broker

Examine your service providers. Is the broker offering you the cheapest execution? Or is it one that not only has stable execution tools that fit your needs, but also has a desk or individual who is assigned to you and will pick up the phone when you need to place that order in person or resolve an execution problem? Are you covered when, for whatever reason, you have a large position on in the market and your data feed and execution platform are down? What is your backup in this eventuality? Without this, you may find your inexpensive broker has suddenly become extremely expensive, indeed.

If you are trading futures and options through a Futures Commission Merchant (FCM), are your funds segregated from the clearing institution? Under U.S. regulations, customer funds must be segregated from the broker. This means that in the case of the failure of the FCM—as in the case of the sudden collapse of REFCO in 2005—your funds are protected. Unlike customers of Refco Overseas Ltd. and Refco Forex, not a single customer of Refco, Inc. suffered losses or an interruption in trading due to the collapse of the firm. Before the failure, Refco, Inc. was the largest FCM on the Chicago Mercantile Exchange with over 200,000 customer accounts. Size is not health.

Any large broker will inevitably have complaints filed against it, but the frequency and nature of complaints can shed light on the culture of your clearing partner. (This was the case in Refco status reports.) They can be found under BASIC on the National Futures Association's web site at www.nfa.futures.org.

Additionally, FCMs must file monthly financial reports with the CFTC's Division of Clearing and Intermediary Oversight (DCIO).[6] This tells us their exchange membership and financial status, including customer capital reserves.

Similarly, a brokerage firm may be researched through Broker Check on the Financial Industry Regulatory Authority's (FINRA) web site, www.finra.org.

Execution Risk

For both the professional and the serious retail trader, the executing broker is the major link in the chain of risk control. Mistakes will always happen when people and machines meet. This cannot ever be eliminated, but we can minimize the likelihood. What happens when your Internet line is down and you have a position on that needs to be canceled, closed, or changed? The market is moving fast, you know exactly what needs to be done, and your Internet-only broker has a service line in a remote call center you need to get through to first before you can talk to anyone about that order. Not only have those cheap rates suddenly become very expensive, but your risk meter has moved into the red. You are not in control. Speak to any trader on a professional executing desk and not only are slippage and execution efficiency critical to their edge for success, but also the ability to immediately address an execution problem. Just as in market event scenario building, think through trade execution blunders and problems before they happen. Address the problem before the fact, not after. Stuff *does* happen.

Infotainment Risk

There is, believe it or not, a risk of trading as entertainment—free data, free charting, technical indicators—that is, a side of speculation that introduces external event risk and can distract the best of us from the task at hand, just as those sitcoms on television may have distracted you from your homework as a kid. (No doubt you also told your Mom, "But it's educational TV!") This leads us to the consideration of information and data risk. What is real information and what is not? Examining the tools of your trade and sorting out the distractions from the essentials will keep you focused on your market perspective.

Where do you get your data? Fortunately, in most all liquid markets data quality has greatly improved over the past decade and is of excellent grade from established data vendors. However, if you are using broker-supplied data, do you understand exactly where and how the data is generated? Is it directly from an exchange, or from a separate data provider? Or is your executing broker, as in the case of some foreign exchange brokers, supplying its own feed for your "free" trading where you pay *only* the spread (the broker's spread, that is, on its supplied data)? Does the source fit your purpose and needs? If not, there is a disconnect and your risk could be increased.

Many of us consider information beyond simply data (and the visual patterns data creates) to enter a trade. Have we evaluated our information sources—news feeds, daily media? What about reports? Is this good information? Is it noise? Does the daily trader buzz (much of it out there to get us to trade) unduly influence us? Do we find ourselves reacting to every sound-bite coming over the airwaves? Can we step back from ourselves and see how we react to information? Ask yourself, "Is this a distraction increasing my risk?" Does the market-related information we consume enhance our trading methods or is it just more entertainment? If so, our risk is increased.

There are skilled forces at work in competition for our attention and actions. It is an industry in which we must participate with care, if at all. Finally, often it is not the loudest information out there, but the information in the cracks, sometimes far behind the story, and deduced information that is the most valuable for our trading decisions.

Event Risk

Event risk, just as all operational risk, is something we can never completely measure but must always anticipate. Events that have nothing to do with the surroundings you can control will have an impact on your trade. This is a risk that belongs to any high-skill endeavor, similar to sports. Anyone who plays a team sport knows that there are thousands of little events in the game each one of which can make or break the overall success. Many times, they are things completely outside of players' control. A golf ball hitting a rock the kids threw onto the green, a sudden rain—all are external. Remember that many of the money management schemes mentioned above cannot take into account the likelihood of external event risks, and surely not trading systems built on gaming rules, which in turn were built on rules of large amounts of fixed numerical data occurrences.

CHANGING THE RULES IN THE MIDDLE OF THE GAME The rules of the game could be changed at any moment, as well. This, too, is event risk. As an anecdote: The rules were suddenly changed during the 1980 panic in the silver market, which was triggered by the Hunt Brothers Squeeze. What happened is that in response to the havoc created by the squeeze (especially for powerful interests who were caught very short on the silver market) there was a sudden introduction of the "Silver Rule 7" restricting the purchase of silver on margin, which resulted in, essentially, a liquidation-only market. The silver market crashed within days. The rules suddenly and unexpectedly changed and the game was over.

The Losing Trade

As previously mentioned, Taleb's ninth rule was to read every book by traders to study where they lost money. "You will learn nothing relevant from their profits (the markets adjust). You will learn from their losses."[7] I'll now present a trade that I learned from immensely.

It was the greatest of all trades, teaching me more than thousands of dollars' worth of courses, books, and lectures. My account was well up for

FIGURE 9.1 Daily Coffee, 1997
Source: Genesis Financial Technologies, Inc.

the year, and the previous year a long options-only strategy allowed me the financial capital to venture into the futures markets. I read everything I could possible find—the newsletters, trading manuals, and so forth.

After doing well in the then Deutchmark futures contract (probably not understanding why I was doing well), I wanted to venture into other markets with my newfound "knowledge." In hindsight, there was an ego-driven consideration. I wanted to prove (show off to whom?) that my system could trade more than just Deutschmark futures and options against the U.S. dollar. To short the coffee market was my next mark. From the start, I broke Taleb's first risk rule. I did not understand what I was trading and I was the sitting duck. (But I had read in all those books and newsletters that a good system works in *all* markets!)

On May 15, Coffee made new highs and the following day presented what we know as an inside day (see Figure 9.1). The contract size (and associated tick value) was much greater than the Deutschmark contract. I entered the usual number of contracts on the sell side. Another risk rule broken: Not only did I not understand the market, and as we will soon see, the exchange (house) rules of the market, I had no proper concept or idea of sound equity-to-margin rules (let alone volatility considerations of the market!). And for anyone who has read along this far, or even has

FIGURE 9.2 Daily Coffee,1997. Coffee Remains in a Bullish Trend Where Probes Lower are Met with Buying.
Source: Genesis Financial Technologies, Inc..

some experience in the market, a glance at this chart tells of the precarious position any short seller is getting into! At this point, I was proud of my trading prowess. Not only had the market closed down for the day, but I had sold at the very top range of price.

On the 19th, the market closed down, settling at the lows. My account was rapidly growing in just a few short days and the market was going my way. But then over the next days, the market recovered to just above my entry, as seen in Figure 9.2.

Then on that Friday, May 23, the market again closed on a slightly weak note as we also see in Figure 9.2. The position was back in the black so I added to the short. The short-term candlestick pattern was again negative for the bulls (with the market closing near the low for the trading session) and I had read that you must let your profits run and not take tiny profits. And it had worked the last time I traded against this daily pattern. Those were the rules of trading. I was in a profit. "Do not let a little market noise shake you out. Let profits run. . . ." *That is what I keep reading in all the books*, I thought.

After market close, I read a report about freezing conditions in South America and what that might mean for the Coffee market. It would be extremely bullish, creating shortages of coffee. Then I found a quote by a floor trader saying that was nonsense and it is summertime—which is exactly what I wanted to hear! (Reality is that it was *wintertime* south of the Equator.) Next risk rule broken: seeking out *bad information* to support wished-for assumptions. I held onto that information—the news reports did not know what they were talking about. My account was now fully loaded with short Coffee contracts. I could let the profits run. Yet I was about to be roasted (pun *intended*) on Monday morning.

Oh, and another thing: I had just canceled my data feed and was now trading off free exchange charting and broker updates. Why pay for data when you can get it free! Another rule broken: a big position on in the market, but no way to reasonably monitor it. My data did not fit my real needs.

Monday morning, stepping out of the shower, clutching a large towel and dripping wet, I answered the telephone. It was my broker. Coffee was called to open up around 2,000 points (or ticks) as I recall. I was not only totally wet, but completely under water. I blurted something like there would be a lock limit and that I would not be able to do anything anyway. He answered, "There are no price limits in the front month." I realized at that instant that I knew *nothing*. I asked him when the market would open. He said "in about 30 minutes." I told him I needed to think about what this means and I would get right back to him.

Here I had broken a series of five rules:

1. I did not understand what I was trading—neither leverage, the market, the contract, nor the exchange rules of the contract—let alone having an understanding of the difference between prevailing price trends and short-term price noise.
2. I had no concept of money management and was completely overleveraged relative to the account size.
3. My motivation for trading was ego-based instead of based in any reality of the opportunity or market. This was trader-imposed market risk.
4. I had no conception that what did happen *could even happen*.
5. When entering the trade I had no plan other than profitability.

Hanging up the phone, one thing was now clear in my mind. I was in way over my head and, no matter what, I would have to be out of the position before the end of the day.

I called a friend and told him what happened. He suggested that I hedge it with options. Or do a "Texas hedge," he said (buying a position in the opposite direction in a different delivery month), which was not possible anyway as the back months were locked-limit (not to mention that it was not a hedging strategy and would increase my risk). Thankfully, my immediate thought was that I was in a trade I had no business being in, and that if I now needed to hedge it to survive, where I obviously did not even know what I was doing, chances were I would make a bigger mess of the trade. (In other words, if you need to start introducing a hedging strategy after the fact, you probably should not be in the trade anyway.) I told him I had to exit the position. "But one thing," I said, "I'll try to exit during a possible intraday pullback." I asked him if I could call him at 15-minute intervals for a price update. (I had this market exposure and no data!)

I then called my broker and closed out all other positions in other markets to increase the margin available in the account. I was battening down the hatches. It was a matter of survival. I told him I would exit Coffee today and asked him if I could call during the day for quotes.

By 12:15, the market was pulling back near to the open. I then told my broker to buy all contracts at market. I was out of the position and my account was down over 45 percent. Months of gains wiped out in a few hours. The market closed that day at the top of the range and the next day it opened up another 4000 points.

Two days later, I called my broker and thanked him for his help. He said that the desk was nervous but rooting for me and that I did just great. "Great?" I said. "I practically blew out an account in one day on a massively stupid trade!" "Oh, no," he said, "I had another client who was in the same boat. He held on, thinking the market would come back the next day. He is gone."

In this case, the market went where no one could imagine, adhering to Taleb's fifth rule: "The markets will follow the path to hurt the highest number of hedgers. The best hedges are those you are the only one to put on." See Figure 9.3.

An Example of a Well-Managed Trade

Do your homework, and bring back the change.
—Mothers everywhere

Most often things do come down to the simplest (not most simplistic) rules of life. Doing our homework and keeping our rules simple enough that we thoroughly understand them can bring us the highest rewards.

Based on your homework, you have decided to purchase an equity. Projected earnings are a forecast and not always a basis of decision making, but you have been following the stock for a few months and are familiar with the cyclical nature of the industry. There is currently a negative news cycle around the industry and little published coverage. This information is not important to you now as price structure is alerting you to possible

FIGURE 9.3 Coffee, May 1997, Market on the Run
Source: Genesis Financial Technologies, Inc.

change on the horizon. However, with this purchase you are prepared for a high level of volatility in both directions. This volatility is not only an indicator of change, but may be an opportunity for trade entry.

Convergence of Structure

What is the reality of the price action? What is the pattern structure of the market? What indicators—price, pattern, indicators, sentiment—come together to support this trade? The equity is still in a downward trend. However, this is a stock you want to own based on your homework, and now you've identified that it is oscillating into a snake pattern over eight weeks around a multiyear S&R range. This is a key price area and a trigger to take a closer look

After the up day on January 23, 2009, you buy at market at 86.90. Aware of the still-downward trend, you allocate .625 percent of your portfolio to this trade—$\frac{1}{4}$ of the total amount (2.5% of your total portfolio) you wish to commit to this trade—that is, if the market continues to confirm with further trade triggers in support of your analysis and homework. The higher the total percentage commitment to a position, the more aggressive the strategy. There are times to be aggressive, depending on various risk considerations

FIGURE 9.4 Anonymous Equity in the Phase of the Snake with Low Volatility at Multiyear S&R after Entropy Vacuum Fall
Source: Copyright 2010 Bloomberg Financial LP.

mentioned above. For now, this relatively less aggressive stance is your plan. Before execution, you work through scenarios and identify what could go wrong with the trade. You consider price levels where you would exit based on how much you want to risk and a pattern that would invalidate your initial entry trigger. See Figure 9.4.

You may want to own this stock, but the trend is down until it is not.

If the market closes one dollar below the current support range of 80.00, you will close the position for an estimated loss of .X percent of your total account equity. If an additional pattern emerges supporting your pattern analysis, you will add another X number of shares depending upon the price. You have done your homework. You have a fixed money management plan for the position and a trade trigger plan.

You have identified your acceptable loss and if the market were to gap down below your stop-loss range, your allocation to the trade is quite low. Risk is never eliminated, but merely minimized.

Over the next weeks, the market retraces to the top of the recent range. (See Figure 9.5.) You reevaluate, but do not add. Why not, if the market is going up? Nothing has changed. You entered the position into the lower

Buy Day No. 1

Adam 1 and Adam 2 ???

Multi year S&R level

Jul 31   Aug 15   Aug 29   Sep 15   Sep 30   Oct 15   Oct 31   Nov 14   Nov 28   Dec 15   Dec 31   Jan 15   Jan 30
                                                  2008   2009
              Daily 11/7/05 to 11/8/10   Copyright 2010 Bloomberg Finance L.P.   07-Nov-2010 11:01:54

FIGURE 9.5 Anonymous Equity
Source: Copyright 2010 Bloomberg Financial LP.

range of the band and there is still no price breakout. In short, even if the market is going up in this short time, there is no additional buy signal, no trade trigger.

As seen in Figure 9.6, over the next days the market retraces down again. The price indecision in a still-downward market makes you a bit nervous. You reevaluate the position and your original entry plan. You consider raising your stop level to the entry price. You ask yourself, "What has changed since trade entry?" Nothing. Your exposure to the position is still quite low. Is time a risk factor in this trade? No. Based on your reevaluation, you keep your stop at the same level.

Weeks later, in late March, you note that the market has a wide range day and closes above the price range. (See Figure 9.7.) The next day, you want to follow your plan and enter the market within the range of the previous day, adding the planned amount of X to your position, allocating half of your total planned commitment to this trade. That evening, you check reports on the equity and do not find news or chatter of note. The only thing you read is that an industry analyst has come out with a hold recommendation—not market-moving information. The next day, the market opens below the close of the up day. You follow your plan and, late in the day, you purchase at 106.00 in what proves to be the middle

FIGURE 9.6 Anonymous Equity

of the trading range. You paid more that you wanted, but your plan was to add to the position on a strong buy pattern trigger, and this was it. You followed your plan of action. Your average price is now 96.45.

You put a stop at 84.30, just below the low of March 10, thinking that the market may close the gap, and if your pattern analysis is correct, it should not close below the low of the swing down. If it does, it would negate the buy signal and the conditions prompting the second buy trigger would no longer exist.

Over the next days the market is quiet and there is a brief return ("kiss" pattern) to the breakout level (see Figure 9.7). You reevaluate the position and your reasons for entering. The trade still has its foundation, but you think to yourself that you could have had the equity for less if you had allowed yourself to attempt to buy on a pullback. However, the possibility that this would not happen and the regret that you would not have been able to enter at this range is the price you were willing to pay. You were prepared for the likelihood of another test down, maybe even back into the S&R range, but not willing to risk the opportunity to add to your position at these levels, if your longer term analysis of a cycle shift is right.

On April 2, we have the lightning bolt pattern where the market gapped open above the previous close and above the recent S&R range.

FIGURE 9.7 Confirmation of the Eve Phase of the Pattern and a Return to the Breakup Range
Source: Copyright 2010 Bloomberg Financial LP.

This completes what may be the cycle bottom pattern. Following your plan, you now add the third block to this position and are filled during the day at 111.20 and your average price is now 101.36.

You put a stop for the entire position below the swing low day of April 1 at 82.50. If your pattern analysis is correct, the market should not return to this low. If it does, your loss is still kept to a minimum, a small fraction of your portfolio, and you can reevaluate.

On May 4, the market makes new period highs. You have three-quarters of your total commitment (now only 1.87 percent of your total equity) to this position and are now willing to risk regret if the market continues up without your full position. Based on the new strength of the market, you raise your stop loss orders to right below the resistance range around 105.00 (see Figure 9.8).

At this point there is excitement in the market as we've had a price run-up of over 50 percent from the lows in this household brand. Further, you've now had an over 30 percent return on your current position. You step back and reevaluate the position again. There is no trigger to add to your position. You raise your sell stop orders to 110.00. Reviewing your

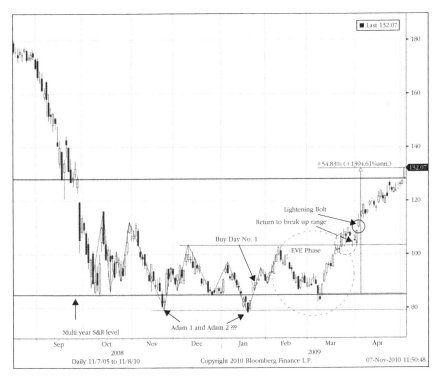

FIGURE 9.8 Continuation and New Period Highs
Source: Copyright 2010 Bloomberg Financial LP.

charts you note something: The market has closed a price gap from September 2008 and now here we are at this price level again. You anticipate that some selling may come in—especially from the technically oriented trading community. If so, this may present a buying opportunity on an equity you still want to purchase. Your average purchase price is around 101. Your plan has been followed and over the past two months you have built a position of just under 2 percent of your portfolio. You put in an order for the final block of shares at 121.00 on anticipation of a pullback to return to the recent break around this key price range. You place a stop for your entire position below the 40-period EMA at 116.00. On May 13 you are filled and the market closes at the low of the day. You expect the market will continue down and that this may have been the end of the rally. You follow your plan and keep your sell stop for the entire position at 116.00.

You note that there are still few buy recommendations on this equity and expect to be taken out of the market in the next days or weeks. Instead, the market proves itself to be in a strong upward trend (see Figure 9.9).

FIGURE 9.9 Continuation after the Lightning Bolt Triggers
Source: Copyright 2010 Bloomberg Financial LP.

Volatility Appears in the Valley of the Kings

Throughout the trade you employ the same market structure analysis, pattern analysis, and scenario building to manage the life of the trade. You have used the simple pattern-recognition tools of S&R, swing identification, and an EMA to quickly and visually determine the health of the trend. This has kept you in the trade for longer than you anticipated. It has been over a year.

In late 2009, you again reevaluate your reasoning for entering the investment. The company has done better than you anticipated and the technical strength of the market is still intact. Twice the market makes a brief swing low below the 40-period EMA. This is now a swing low range and a support range. You move your stop for ½ of the position below this swing low and the 40 EMA and ½ below the September 2009 price gap at 172.00.

The market sees new highs in December and you raise your highest stop to below the 40 EMA and the market fills the sell stops on January 28 at 202.30 for over a 90 percent return on the portion realized. (See Figure 9.10.) The market still continues higher than you ever expected. You consider buying back what you just sold as you see the market break up into ever-higher highs in the new year (see Figure 9.11). You again reevaluate and determine that not only is the market now in an unhealthy price progression, but your original reasons for buying the stock no longer hold,

FIGURE 9.10 A King of a Market Makes a Pause
Source: Copyright 2010 Bloomberg Financial LP.

and if you did not hold it already, you certainly would not be buying as it would be like chasing a speeding train. So why buy more now? You put away the idea and raise your stop to 219.00 for the rest of the position, below the 40 EMA and swing low around 220.00.

The Unexpected Strikes: Market Kryptonite

On May 6, 2010, the market experiences the *flash crash*: an external operational risk that never happened before and could not be built into any backward-looking VaR model. (In fact, the possibility of the events leading to a 600 point drop in 5 minutes—and over 1000 points during the day—was not even imagined possible by regulators or market participants.) Your sell stop orders are filled, not at 220.00 but at 211.50! You are more than a bit shocked and think back to the day when you flirted with the idea of adding to your position as it gapped up near 260. You are relieved that you held to the plan based on your homework in both buying and selling and not on the emotions in reaction to the market. Your average buy price was 106.25 and your average selling price was 206.90, a 95 percent return on the position.

The flash crash could have happened at any time during the lift of the trade. In spite of this, every aspect of management—risk management, money

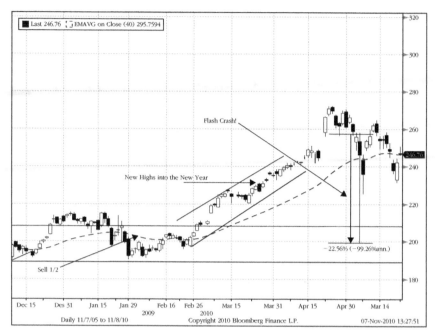

FIGURE 9.11 The Impossible Happens! May 6, 2010 "Flash Crash"
Source: Copyright 2010 Bloomberg Financial LP.

management, trade management, event management, information management, operational management, and most importantly, personal management—all greatly enhanced your overall successful trading performance.

Conclusion

Many of the ideas presented here are perhaps an unconventional approach to thinking about the markets and pattern recognition, or even go against the grain of conventional thought. But if you come away from this book with just a few *good* ideas that help you develop your own trading strategies into a method that fits your risk appetite and market approach, it has been a successful read.

With some of the risk-measurement metrics mentioned here, we can properly monitor our trades and have honest statistically based insight into our performance. Methods and rituals for doing your homework and for scenario building, clearly defining the trade triggers, having a plan of action, and controlling operational and trader-imposed risk not only will help us become very good and profitable traders over time, but will also bring us a little closer to our Holy Grail—or our own imaginary Dulcinea del Toboso.

Notes

Chapter 1 Perception and Pattern

1. www.cftc.gov/MarketReports/CommitmentsofTraders/index.htm.
2. Cynthia Angell and Clare D. Rowley, *FDIC: Summer Outlook 2006* (www.fdic. gov/bank/analytical/regional/ro20062q/na/2006_summer04.html).
3. Ibid.
4. Ibid.

Chapter 2 Visualizing the Concept of What Makes a Price

1. Benoit B. Mandelbrot, *The (Mis)Behaviour of Markets: A Fractal View of Risk, Ruin and Reward* (London: Profile Books Ltd., 2004), 28.
2. Scott Patternson, *The Quants: How a New Breed of Math Whizzes Conquered Wall Street and Nearly Destroyed It* (New York: Crown Business, 2010), 195–196.
3. Richard H. Thaler, *The Winner's Curse: Paradoxes and Anomalies of Economic Life* (Princeton University Press, 1992), 150.
4. Ibid.
5. Robert A. Olsen, "Cognitive Dissonance: The Problem Facing Behavioral Finance," *Journal of Behavioral Finance*, 9, no. 1 (2008): 1–4.
6. State Street Corporation, *Vision Focus: Research-Driven Strategies in Turbulent Markets* (September 2009).

Chapter 4 A Downside Reversal

1. Thomas Bulfinch, *The Age of Fable* (New York: Lothrop, Lee & Shepard, 1894), 191.
2. Ibid., p. 326.
3. business.timesonline.co.uk/tol/.../banking_and.../article6797794.ece.

4. Ibid.
5. Dina El Boghdady and David Cho, "U.S. Agencies Trying to Recoup Mortgage Scam Losses Linked to Taylor Bea," *Washington Post* Staff Writer, June 19, 2010.
6. Floyd Norris, *New York Times*, August 31, 2007 (http://select.nytimes.com/2007/08/31/business/31norris.html?_r=1&ref=colonial-bancgroup-inc).
7. Ibid.

Chapter 5   Price and Repeating Order

1. Chaos theory holds that slight changes in a system, or minor change in the initial conditions, can have an outsized effect or consequence. See "the butterfly effect."
2. The theory of market structure is that it moves up and down in the structure of a series of waves based on the numerical Fibonacci sequence found in nature.
3. The theory that market cycles follow predictive patterns of price and time that follow logical geometric rules.
4. www.bachelierfinance.org/category/the-society.
5. www-groups.dcs.st-and.ac.uk/~history/Biographies/Bachelier.html.
6. Benoit Mandelbrot, "How Fractals Can Explain What's Wrong with Wall Street," *Scientific American*, September 15, 2008 (www.scientificamerican.com/article.cfm?id=multifractals-explain-wall-street&page=2).
7. Hurst worked on the engineering of a Nile dam and divided the Nile data into segments and examined the logarithmic range and scale of each segment in comparison to the number of total segments, the Hurst exponent.
8. Sydney Opera House, "Sydney Opera House: Utzon Design Principles," Sydney, Australia, May 2002, 16.
9. Ibid.

Chapter 6   Into the Valley of the Kings and the Place of Truth

1. www.thebanmappingproject.com/articles/article_2.2.html.
2. Ibid.
3. Ibid.

Chapter 7   Market Weather

1. http://science.nasa.gov/science-news/science-at-nasa/2006/10mar_storm-warning/.
2. www.weatherquestions.com/What_causes_lightning.htm.
3. www.nssl.noaa.gov/primer/lightning/ltg_basics.html.

Chapter 8   Inside Market Cycles

1. Alan S. Farley, *The Master Swing Trader* (New York: McGraw-Hill, 2001), 71.

Chapter 9   Managing Risk with Applied Trading Tactics

1. Hersh Sheffrin, *Beyond Greed and Fear: Understanding Behavior Finance and the Psychology of Investing* (Harvard Business School Press, 2000), 57.
2. Ralph Vince, *The Mathematics of Money Management: Risk Analysis Techniques for Traders* (New York: John Wiley, 1992).
3. Ralph Vince, *The Leverage Space Trading Model: Reconciling Portfolio Management Strategies and Economic Theory* (Hoboken, N.J.: John Wiley & Sons, 2009).
4. "Against Value-at-Risk: Nassim Taleb Replies to Philippe Jorion," 1997 (www.fooledbyrandomness.com/jorion.html).
5. www.basel-ii-accord.com/Basel_ii_644_to_682_Operational_Risk.htm.
6. www.cftc.gov/MarketReports/FinancialDataforFCMs/index.htm.
7. "Against Value-at-Risk: Nassim Taleb Replies to Philippe Jorion," 1997 (www.fooledbyrandomness.com/jorion.html).

Index

Printed and bound by CPI Group (UK) Ltd, Croydon, CR0 4YY

16/04/2025

14658513-0004